VANCE ROUSH

HIGH-GROWTH
FUNDRAISING
THE **SILICON VALLEY** WAY

UNLOCKING
STOCK, CRYPTO, AND **MORE**
FOR YOUR NONPROFIT, CHURCH, OR SCHOOL

WILEY

For general information on our other products and services or for technical support, please contact our Customer Care Department within the United States at (800) 762-2974, outside the United States at (317) 572-3993 or fax (317) 572-4002.

Wiley also publishes its books in a variety of electronic formats. Some content that appears in print may not be available in electronic formats. For more information about Wiley products, visit our website at www.wiley.com.

Library of Congress Cataloging-in-Publication Data is Available:

ISBN: 9781394152384 (cloth)
ISBN: 9781394152391 (ePub)
ISBN: 9781394152407 (ePDF)

Cover Design: Wiley
Cover Image: Flower: © Tetiana Saranchuk/Getty Images
Roots: © engabito/Getty Images

SKY10041698_012323

This book is dedicated to my wife and mother of our four children, Kim Roush. My partner and best friend. We realized early in our marriage that we would build a life based on biblical generosity, because we believe that the life of the generous gets larger and larger. Your generosity inspires me and propels me into my calling. Thank you.

Contents

Contents

Foreword

"To remain static is to lose ground."

Bill Hewlett and David Packard

Being situated and pastoring now for over a decade in Silicon Valley, which is undisputedly the leading ecosystem globally for innovation, I can certainly attest to the unique atmosphere of optimism that exists here. Now admittedly, "here" is somewhat of an elusive concept because there is no city or suburb named Silicon Valley, which makes it difficult to pinpoint on a map. That's because Silicon Valley isn't actually a location as much as it's a mindset or *way* of approaching things. At best we could arguably orient the birthplace of Silicon Valley at 367 Addison Avenue, Palo Alto, California, which is the iconic garage location and start-up space of Hewlett-Packard. However, more than the birthplace of a computing and technology company, what began in that space was a *way* of approaching both obstacles and opportunities with innovation. This my friends, is the Silicon Valley Way.

You see, as stated at the beginning of this foreword, remaining static is a sure way to lose ground especially, when it comes to raising capital or fundraising for a new project or venture. In fact, I have discovered that the "pitch" is merely one part of the process. More than simply revealing a desired destination or communicating a new and exciting initiative, casting the vision is a catalytic moment that unlocks belief, inspires generosity, and also releases creativity. However, the success of a pitch or vision cast can't be measured solely by the moment on the microphone. A large part of its success is found in the innovative tools or new processes you can provide to see capital released effectively toward your cause. Whether you're a CEO, founder, pastor, or leader, the potency of your vision is either limited or unlocked by the pathways you provide.

Many charitable organizations like the church can easily find themselves stalled by antiquated traditions or systems that fail to serve a new generation of donors and givers. For example, many modern high-growth companies don't follow traditional compensation methods for employees. Instead, we find a lot of employees, for tax and growth purposes, opting for a larger stock component over cash to their compensation package. The organization that fails to innovate new ways to cater for this new wave of workforce also potentially fails to maximize their impact when raising funds. This is what I have learned from Vance Roush as we have partnered together in dozens of initiatives over the past decade. Vance's experience in straddling both the faith and fintech space lends him a unique perspective on how to utilize a Silicon Valley approach to accelerating nonprofit organizations that rely on the generosity of donors. As an ordained minister and company founder, Vance brings a wealth of wisdom to the capital raising table. His insights are not mere theories but proven practices over time that have resulted in tens of millions of dollars unlocked for kingdom and charitable advancement.

I truly believe this book will serve as an essential tool for any leader desiring to maximize their impact when fundraising or finding a new approach to unlocking the potential within their organization. Vance has a unique capability of helping leaders see the potential opportunities that exist within real-world problems. As a prolific practitioner of generosity himself, Vance is a leading voice in creating frictionless pathways for giving, serving both the organization and the donor simultaneously. I believe this resource will serve you through the many growth stages of your organization and help maximize your impact and influence.

—Adam Smallcombe, Global Lead Pastor, VIVE Church
Silicon Valley

Preface

I am incredibly excited to share this book with you, especially if you are a fundraiser, pastor, development director, nonprofit founder, or have a dream in your heart to make an impact on the world and want to raise philanthropic funds to resource it. Whatever the case may be, I feel uniquely qualified to provide stories, stats, strategies, and practical tactics to give you great guidance and courage to unlock generosity for your cause.

I am so passionate about the first principles of generosity, and how it enlarges peoples' lives, that I started a whole company with a mission to inspire the world to give. Overflow.co is building the infrastructure that makes generosity frictionless across every major asset class.

Here is an article I posted on LinkedIn when I launched the company in July 2020 entitled "Why I Started a Fintech Company Focused on Generosity":

> Last summer I was sitting in our living room in San Jose with a couple of friends sharing with them a vision to build the future of generosity. We started mind mapping, specifically meditating on an ancient Proverb: The world of the generous gets larger and larger (Proverbs 11:24 MSG). This verse has been a foundation, first principle in my marriage, and one my wife and I have experienced the power of

within our church community. A revelation that has revolutionized
our life, and one that has gripped many of our closest friends.

As we unpacked this verse further in our brainstorming session,
we created bubbles around words like FRAGRANCE, EXTRA-
VAGANT, and OVER THE TOP. For Kim and [me], we have been
on both the receiving and the giving side of generosity. We grew up as
first-generation Asian Americans in a low- to middle-class suburb of
Seattle called Kent. A city full of immigrants, we were immersed in
the hustle with incredible parents who did everything they could
to provide us an opportunity to "make it." I remember many days
my dad coming home late after a double shift in the grueling
aerospace industry and smelling the sweat and fumes from the factory
on his clothes. That's when I experienced that generosity had a
FRAGRANCE and it smells like sacrifice.

With that energy, I followed in my parents footsteps to work all
throughout high school and college, determined to be able to pay
tuition and board at the University of Washington, without incurring
any debt. Dozens of jobs and scholarship applications later, I finally
received my first scholarship at the end of Sophomore year, with many
that followed, which would end up paying for the rest of my college
tuition, rent, books & more! Even though these were considered
"merit-based," I definitely didn't feel like I deserved it. This "free
money" felt EXTRAVAGANT, and in reflection, was transformative
in unlocking opportunities, like study abroad, because I was no longer
tied down with 3 jobs.

Post graduation, Kim and I (newlyweds at the time) moved to
Silicon Valley to start our careers in tech (Google) and education
(Teach for America). As a "Noogler" in 2011, I definitely went in
expectant, due to all the articles I read about Google's perks, but as
I toured the campus on orientation day I was still completely taken
aback by the abundance of food and generosity with services such as
massages, dry cleaning, & G-Buses that picked you up anywhere in the
Bay Area. All I could think was that this was OVER THE TOP.

I know some have a similar journey to me but many more don't. I also know that each life-changing opportunity I have been blessed with was ultimately a result of generosity. Everyone won't have the chance to attend a 4-year university or to study abroad or to work at a top tech company, but everyone should have the chance to experience generosity. The FRAGRANT, EXTRAVAGANT, and OVER THE TOP kind.

We believe we have been given so much, and can't help but grow in the conviction and responsibility to give back, unlocking opportunities and access for others. Giving rooted in gratitude is what we call giving out of the Overflow. It has nothing to do with what's in your bank balance and what you don't have, but everything to do with recognizing what you've been given and what you do have. From that place, our mission is to inspire the world to give.

We're starting with stock-based giving, but not stopping there. We will unlock every major asset class until anyone, anywhere can give anything to the people & causes they care about so that every human being will experience the enlarged life of the generous. The Proverbs 11:24 life.

Alongside my career in technology which started at Google, Kim and I have also had the privilege of being on the founding team of a church in the Silicon Valley called VIVE Church. Overflow is at the intersection of my passion for technology and our calling to serve in our community. Ultimately what I have found is that churches, charities, and the wider nonprofit sector have lagged behind in technology, which greatly inhibits the possibilities for resources to be truly unlocked that can accelerate important missions and visions. The gap is so great and personal to me, especially living in the Silicon Valley, where I see so much talent, technology, and innovation being focused on the for-profit space. For example, Google built ads that are contextual to your search; Amazon made it easy to buy anything online and it would show up within your doorstep within days if not hours; Uber made it possible to have your own driver with the click of a button on your phone. I'm immersed in a region that has birthed incredible innovation, but found myself stuck as an executive pastor and chief financial officer of a church not even able to receive a stock donation in our brokerage account without involving physical forms and fax machines.

So now I have dedicated my life to building technology and user experiences on the web to unlock generosity for organizations that are changing the world. The same energy Tesla has for building a future that will have autonomous vehicles, the same energy SpaceX has for colonizing Mars, is the same energy my team and I have for creating a future where anyone can give anything to any organization in the world at any time. We want to build the spaceships for generosity. Not only because it will resource important causes, but it is also transformative for the giver. When someone becomes a consistent giver, they find purpose, grow in empathy, and scientifically become happier. Generosity enlarges our world.

My hope for this book is that it would remove limitations in your fundraising endeavors. I want to show you through anecdotes, but also empirically, that there has never been so many available resources for fundraisers to capitalize on. These resources belong to the ones with bold vision, courage, and the context to understand the world we currently live in: a world centered on convenience, hungry for meaning, and thirsty for identity within community.

The tactics and the playbooks that I provide in this book at the time of writing this have helped nearly 400 top churches, charities, and educational institutions, and we at Overflow have unlocked tens of millions in net new value that likely otherwise wouldn't have existed. We won't stop building out the tools and playbooks necessary until every org is resourced with what they need to accomplish their mission. There are still communities who need clean water, cities that need housing, people who need food, neighborhoods that need faith, and so many more pressing problems that can be solved through human ingenuity, focus, and the sufficient amount of finances. There is more than enough capital, but not enough education on how to position your organization to receive that capital. We hope this book inspires and equips you on your journey to be the most effective fundraiser you can be.

In this book, we take a unique angle by drawing parallels between philanthropic fundraising and Silicon Valley venture capital (VC) fundraising. Philanthropic fundraising can definitely take a note from start-up founders and their fundraising process and mentality. As a VC-backed founder myself, I am excited to use this mentality to unlock fresh and new ways you can be empowered with in the fundraising environment we are in today.

Let's dive in!

Acknowledgments

I want to acknowledge my church community, VIVE Church. This is the place Kim and I have had the privilege to be on the founding team, serve in many capacities, and have called home for more than a decade. This book, and my company Overflow, was inspired by the incredibly generous community that has been cultivated at VIVE. The sacrificial, extravagant, irrational, and catalytic generosity that is consistently expressed in this church is not normal. It is supernatural, and we have seen it has been a product of the powerful revelation of God and how good He is. How unlimited His resources are. How much of a privilege it is to be used by Him to spread faith, hope, and love. How life giving it is to witness how He can turn money into someone's miracle. Thank you to all the families who have lived out the life of the generous and challenge us each and every year to grow in generosity.

And to our lead pastors, and pioneers of this community, who have now affected tens of thousands all across the globe, Pastors Adam and Keira Smallcombe. One of the best decisions we have ever made in our life was in 2012 when we said yes to the vision God gave you for VIVE Church. Nothing has stretched us more, grown us more, and allowed us to live our best life like building the local church has. It takes leaders with vision, humility, resilience, and BIG faith to build a church like VIVE, which has raised up generations, called people higher into their purpose, released people into their calling, and has forged a pathway for hundreds of families to live a life of faith and first principles that have transformed whole communities. I personally know hundreds of people, including my own family, who are better because of your obedience to God's will and ways. Thank you for living a life beyond yourselves.

To my family. My Mom and Dad, who taught me the importance of living a life of principle. Fundamental truths like work ethic and servant-heartedness are truths you not only taught me but lived out day after day. The sacrifice and love you poured on my brother and me did not go unnoticed, and much of what I have been able to accomplish to date is really built on that foundation that you set.

To my incredible children, Lennox, Emerson, Tatum, and Wesleigh Dior. It's because of each of you that I understand God's generosity toward us. It is clear that each of you are fearfully and wonderfully made. Each of you are unique in your expression of God's beautiful design, and your mother and I are so privileged to steward the vision that you all are. You bring an overflow of joy to our lives.

To my flow fam. There's a special reward for those who are first in, early adopters, and pioneers. At the time of writing this book, we are still very much in the early stages of fulfilling the mission and vision of our company: to inspire the world to give and to build the infrastructure that makes generosity frictionless across every major asset class. Thank you for believing in that vision and carrying that vision with the weight and responsibility that it deserves. When we achieve it together, we know we will have changed the world. Special shoutout to those who have had their footprint on this book. From researching to writing to transcribing, there were specific individuals at Overflow or those who have partnered with Overflow who have made important contributions to this resource, which we hope helps many people. Kingdom Books, Mighty Pursuit, Good Ideas Gayle, Chris Sawyer, and many more. Thank you!

1 | Unlock Unprecedented Amounts of Generosity

November 8, 2019, marked the moment where I decided to dedicate my life to unlocking unprecedented amounts of generosity. To set the stage, it was the day of VIVE Church Vision Gala 2019—our seventh annual fundraising gala as a church. VIVE Church is the church Kim, my wife, and I are on the founding team of based in the Silicon Valley, California.

Many of you who have led, facilitated, or been part of a fundraising gala would know that there are a lot of emotions around this event. There is anticipation around sharing the vision and future initiatives, but at the same time anxiety around if people will respond. There is genuine excitement for those in the room who will be invited to be part of the vision, but at the same time a reluctance to ask for money yet again. There is confidence in the preparation you and your team have put into the event and presentation, but at the same time a cautiousness to not get your hopes up so that you can take the edge off of any potential disappointment. These are the battles that go on in our mind leading up to important events like galas that are mission critical for the year to come.

For us and our leadership team at the church, this was that night. A night that was familiar because we had done this for seven years now. But one that would still require faith because the leader of our organization, Pastor Adam, is one to always push the limits of what is possible.

For context, VIVE Church started in 2012, founded by two Aussies: Pastors Adam and Keira Smallcombe. In 2012, they sold everything in Australia and moved from Sydney to the Silicon Valley with their three little girls and a deep conviction that they would start a church that had the potential to change the world through its message. A church that mobilized a community committed to serving the city, living a lifestyle of generosity, and connecting people to a cause greater than themselves. Through a few divine connections and an exchange on Twitter (another story for another book), we met Pastors Adam and Keira, heard their vision for this church, and Kim and I became the first two members.

In true Silicon Valley start-up fashion, we started the church with seven people in a living room: me, Kim, Pastors Adam and Keira, and their three girls Madiha, Zali, and Zara. What started with seven people in a living room, in just seven years became a few thousand people across 10 physical locations: five in the San Francisco Bay Area, plus Chicago, Austin, Honolulu, Milan, and Rome. The rapid expansion is really a testament to the bold and courageous vision set by our pastors to be a community that was never stagnant but always stretching and growing to further its impact.

The reality is that to expand it requires significant amounts of finances. Similar to how start-ups raise funding from venture capitalists and investors to build innovative breakthrough companies, from the beginning we knew we needed to raise multiple funding rounds to fulfill the vision for our church. The way that we operate as a church is that our vision always exceeds our financial resources. With every single vision gala, the initiatives that we presented were far beyond our resources, capacity, or capability. But every single year we witnessed our incredible community step up, stretch, sacrifice, and give generously toward seeing a bold and audacious vision fulfilled!

VIVE Vision Gala 2020 was no different. These are the initiatives that were presented:

- **VIVE University:** starting a fully accredited college program that will teach everything from the bible to business. A place where the next generation of leaders will be trained, equipped, empowered, and released to make a difference in all spheres of life.
- **VIVE at Home:** an expression of the VIVE Worship experience that will extend into cities where we do not yet have a

physical location. For example, expressions of VIVE were already happening in living rooms within cities such as Madrid, Spain.

- **Project VIVE:** a multiyear capital campaign that went toward saving for a building purchase that would facilitate our church gatherings in Palo Alto, California.
- **Eradicating Medical Debt:** a partnership with a nonprofit, RIP Medical, to eradicate $20 million worth of medical debt in the cities that we serve. We would do this through RIP Medical's innovative program where $1 donated cancels out $100 worth of medical debt for low-income families in need of medical services but don't have the insurance or means to pay for it.

To accomplish the initiatives we presented, that night we would need to raise $2 million above and beyond the community's regular giving. At that time, it was one of the largest asks we had ever had to the community and consistent with our mode of operation to have a vision that exceeded our resources. What I love about that mentality is that it leaves a large gap for people to give. The generosity gap.

After a night of connection, a year-in-review reflection, fancy dinner, climactic vision presentation, and time given for people to respond with giving, it left us with the moment of truth. This is the moment when, as the executive pastor and treasurer on the board, I connect with our finance team as they put together the report on how much money we raised. The way we tally up the committed giving amount is a combination of accounting for the written-in response cards and the donations that came through our online giving platform that night. I call it the moment of truth because each year I have the incredible privilege to deliver the news to our pastors so they can receive it, digest it, and have the information they need to report on it to the church for that upcoming Sunday.

Drum roll, please.

That night, we raised $2.3 million!

This exceeded our goal of $2 million! An incredible act of generosity by the community that would enable us to fulfill all of our vision initiatives for 2020.

Here is where the game changed for me—$1.1 million of that $2.3 million would be in stock donations and facilitated by a new platform I had just built called Overflow.

To understand the significance of this, you must understand that stock donations had never been this significant in our church before. We had one-off stock gifts come in here and there, but at the maximum it represented 5% of total giving for the year. On our biggest giving night of VIVE Church history at that time, for stock donations to represent nearly 50% of the committed amount was a revelation that would set me on a path and passion to see this type of generosity be unlocked for churches, charities, and nonprofit organizations all over the world. It was the moment I realized that unlocking noncash assets would be absolutely key to inspiring unprecedented amounts of generosity within communities everywhere.

The Last Decade of Facilitating Giving Within Churches and Charities

Rewind a little bit. Why did I create this platform for stock donations in the first place, and what is it?

Overflow was an idea birthed out of my own pain point. As the executive pastor and treasurer on the board at VIVE, I had assumed the day-to-day role of chief financial officer (CFO) at that time. This included creating and overseeing processes to receive, manage, and report on giving and charitable donations—a church's primary source of income and finances.

When we started the church, payment platforms were not very advanced, and at the very least the technologies out there like PayPal were not purpose-built for churches or charities. So much of how we processed and managed donations just 10 years ago was very manual. It included cash, checks, outdated online giving widgets with poor user experience, spreadsheets, printing, deposit slips, bank visits, and so on, just to process a few thousand dollars each week. Within the last 10 years, there have been some investments in charitable giving technology platforms and the creation of more seamless online giving experiences for donors. This has made way for more people to turn on recurring donations, automating their giving online, which has been a game changer to unlock generosity and provide more predictability in giving and finances. Additionally, because the giving is inherently online, it's now more possible to automate a lot of the back office tasks that were previously manual, saving precious time and resources for the organization.

Fast forward to March 2020 and the COVID-19 pandemic; it's because of this technology that churches and charities were able to survive. With no in-person gatherings or galas, it was necessary to shift most, if not all, of an organization's giving to online if that organization was going to have resources available to keep going. This means that giving is becoming more automated, recurring, and convenient directly from donor's checking and/or credit accounts.

A report from Blackbaud Institute, a research division of nonprofit cloud software company Blackbaud, found that online giving grew 21% during 2020. As shown in Figure 1.1, Double the Donation (2022) found that across generations, from millennials to boomers, there is a large preference (over 50%) to give online with a credit or debit card.

As this graph shows, online giving is now the predominant preference amongst boomers, Gen X, and millennials.

MILLENNIAL DONORS WORLDWIDE		GEN X DONORS WORLDWIDE		BABY BOOMER DONORS WORLDWIDE	
PREFER TO GIVE		**PREFER TO GIVE**		**PREFER TO GIVE**	
Online (credit/debit card)	55%	Online (credit/debit card)	55%	Online (credit/debit card)	54%
Cash	14%	Bank/Wire Transfer	12%	Direct Mail/Post	19%
Bank/Wire Transfer	11%	Cash	10%	Bank/Wire Transfer	10%
PayPal	9%	PayPal	10%	PayPal	8%
MOST INSPIRED TO GIVE BY		**MOST INSPIRED TO GIVE BY**		**MOST INSPIRED TO GIVE BY**	
Social Media	39%	Social Media	33%	Email	33%
Email	23%	Email	26%	Social Media	19%
Website	20%	Website	19%	Direct Mail/Post	18%
Direct Mail/Post	6%	Direct Mail/Post	9%	Website	16%

Figure 1.1   Cross-generation giving preferences

Source: Double the Donation (2022).

In an Amazon era where as a society we value convenience at a premium, this trend and preference will not slow down. Cash, check, and direct mail to deliver donations will continue to dwindle as the world continues to become increasingly digital.

The Origin Story of Overflow

Experiencing the evolution of how giving and donations are processed in the last decade, alongside my experience in technology (I'm a former Googler and led product at a growth-stage start-up in Palo Alto), provides the context for my perspective of where giving technology needs to go and how it needs to flow. Outside of the processing and merchant fees associated with debit and credit giving online, I was largely happy with how the online giving platform we were using made it easy for people to give via ACH, debit, or credit. One giving channel that made me unhappy, however, was whenever one of our members wanted to give in the form of stock, ETF, IRA, or mutual fund because there was no online platform that made this easy. It had happened several times over the course of my tenure as CFO, and each time it involved following extra work:

- Manual paperwork to be filled out by the donor and/or us.
- Calls to brokerage firms like Charles Schwab and Fidelity to check in on the stock transfer; these firms always had call wait times by the way, which is always frustrating.
- Manual reconciliation of gifts where it wasn't clear who the stock transfer was from so sometimes we didn't know who to thank for the donation!
- The manual creation of acknowledgment letters and additional tax forms to ensure we were IRS-compliant.

Long story short: it was a pain. It also felt like in a lot of ways it was a process and way of giving that was stuck in the stone ages and didn't evolve with the overall online giving trend. The whole process was very foreign to me as a former Google employee who was accustomed to simple digital products that empowered you to do complex tasks with ease.

Typically working at a church or charity means you're under-resourced for all the tasks you need to do, so adding this pain point of processing a stock donation on top of the day-to-day work always led me to secretly wish the donor would just give via check instead. That's embarrassing for me to admit, but if you're reading this and in a position similar to mine, you would have likely thought the same thing if you've experienced the stock donation process! Don't judge me.

My epiphany moment for Overflow was mid-2019 when I was checking in on one of these intended stock donation gifts from one of our donors—a millennial donor who worked at Facebook at the time whose charitable stock transfer had still not come through after months of waiting. I finally asked the donor directly, "Do you have everything you need to complete that gift?" By the way, this is already an awkward interaction to have, and not a position I love to be in. Our heart is that giving doesn't feel like an invoice, rather, one that is a celebration and easy to accomplish. With the genuine pursuit of understanding, I had the conversation and will never forget the response: "Oh, I'm so sorry, Vance, yes, thank you for the church's brokerage information you provided. I actually forwarded the information to my broker at Charles Schwab, and they sent me a link to a form that I need to download, print, fill out physically, and then fax in. I just haven't had a chance to do it yet, but I promise I will get it done!"

At that moment I knew that if you tell a millennial to fax in anything, it's definitely not going to happen.

Who owns a fax machine?

Even if you did, who actually knows how to use it?

Let's say you can figure it out . . . the reality is that most people won't make time for it.

If you can order a bathtub and it's at your door step in two hours because of Amazon Prime, you are most definitely not going to inconvenience yourself by filling out a form and interacting with a brokerage firm to donate. Especially if it's just a few shares of Uber you bought on Robinhood or E-Trade.

And that was my epiphany. If we could remove this friction for the donor and make this stock donation process as easy as an Amazon Prime order, we could potentially unlock unprecedented amounts of generosity. So in October 2019, that's what I set out to do ahead of our VIVE Vision Gala. I partnered with one of my software engineering friends, and we built the first version of Overflow that enabled someone to give stock online without having to fill in paperwork or mess with fax machines. This is the platform that VIVE used that November that facilitated $1.1 million worth of generosity!

It's All About the Experience

So that's principle number one with unlocking generosity. It must be simple and easy! It's a powerful principle that Silicon Valley is built on. Apple, Amazon, Google, and Facebook invest billions of dollars into reducing clicks, personalizing pages, and providing elegant user interfaces and seamless user experiences. This principle enables their products to be accessible and encourages people to use and evangelize their products—because of the experience and ease!

This would be a good time to pause for a moment and go on your donation page and evaluate if it's an Amazon or Apple-like experience. If not, there's probably room for improvement to unlock further generosity. How many people land on your web page and get frustrated because the page is confusing, not mobile optimized, or generally not a great experience? For these reasons, they might even abandon their donation. We know for a fact this happens when it comes to donors who may have the means to give in the form of noncash assets like stocks. Most donate or "ways to give" web pages today point people to email the finance team to "learn more" about how to give stock. Nobody wants to do that.

A Sea Change in Giving

Improvements in user experience for donating online are connected to a macro trend that is leading to a sea change in the way people give generously. Due to the poor user experience of donating stock and, frankly, lack of education and awareness about it, there has been this latent demand for stock donations. To understand what I mean, let's look at donor-advised funds (DAFs) (see Figure 1.2).

You can see here that from 2016 to 2020 there has been a complete explosion of donors contributing charitably to a DAF, primarily through appreciated stock gains. In context, there was an overall total of $471 billion donated in 2020 (Define Financial, 2022), which means DAFs accounted for 10% of all donations!

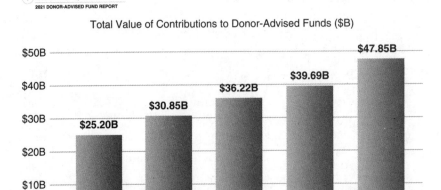

Figure 1.2   Increase in DAFs from 2016 to 2020

Source: National Philanthropic Trust (2021), https://www.nptrust.org/reports/daf-report/, last accessed October 06, 2022.

What Is a Donor-advised Fund?

This is how Fidelity, the largest DAF provider in the world, explains it (Fidelity Charitable, 2022):

> A donor-advised fund, or DAF, is like a charitable investment account for the sole purpose of supporting charitable organizations you care about.
>
> When you contribute cash, securities or other assets to a donor-advised fund at a public charity, like Fidelity Charitable, you are generally eligible to take an immediate tax deduction. Then those funds can be invested for tax-free growth, and you can recommend grants to virtually any IRS-qualified public charity.
>
> You want your charitable donations to be as effective as possible when you give. Donor-advised funds are the fastest growing charitable giving vehicle in the United States because they are one of the easiest and most tax-advantageous ways to give to charity.

The largest DAFs are connected to the major brokerage firms and collectively they have total assets undisbursed within these DAF accounts that amount to over $150 billion! That is $150 billion earmarked for charitable causes that has not yet been distributed.

So why are all those assets sitting in a DAF account and not being distributed and put to work within your nonprofit? User experience and education! When a stockholder is encouraged by their brokerage firm to "donate" some of their appreciated gains from their equity holdings toward their charitable DAF account custodied at the same brokerage firm, they are being educated by their broker on the benefits to do it, and the technology makes it super easy to do. Just a few clicks and you can give stock to your DAF, save on taxes, and now you have this account earmarked for philanthropy.

DAFs prove that people want to donate noncash assets like stock, for many reasons we will get into in a later chapter (specifically Chapter 5), but the main reason why it's not flowing toward your organization directly is because of the lack of education and the friction your website poses for the donor to actually do it. My belief is that through platforms like Overflow, we will accelerate this sea change in giving through technology and unlock unprecedented amounts of generosity.

The phenomena with DAFs is just the tip of the iceberg. The average DAF account holder is 63 years old with a DAF account balance of $167,000. That is not the average American and does not represent the future generation of giving. Through technology, we can increase by 10 times the amount of noncash asset donations by democratizing DAF-like activity for the average American and the next generation. For stocks alone, that would mean that the next $470 billion is ready to be unlocked!

If we include cryptocurrency and the wider Web3 space, that adds another trillion dollar market available for giving. The rise of crypto is really on the back of the larger trend of the democratization of wealth through access to investable assets. Historically, most Americans focused solely on achieving homeownership as their exclusive form of asset ownership outside of their 401k. Today, that has completely shifted. Because of financial technology (or fintech for short), access to many more appreciating assets are now available to the average person—everything from art, wine, collectibles, valuable Jordan sneakers, and yes, NFTs. It used to be that the average millennial would keep 20% of their net worth in investments and 40% in cash within their checking and savings. Due to the increase in access to investments alongside fear of inflation, that ratio has completely flipped with millennials now holding more than 40% of their net worth in investable assets!

The sea change in giving is happening because charitable giving technology advancements, education about the benefits of giving noncash assets, and the allocation of wealth in noncash assets are colliding to create a wave of new giving opportunities! If most people have their wealth in noncash assets now, and we can make it super easy for them to give those assets, it will unlock unprecedented net new giving. Soon, we will see not just $470 billion given in a year to nonprofits, but $1 trillion. That extra $530 billion will not be from donors' checking and savings accounts. It will be donated directly from where they hold their wealth.

Do you want to be part of this sea change in giving so that your organization has the resources it needs to fulfill its mission and vision? Join us in this book to learn about high-growth fundraising, the Silicon Valley way!

2 | Unlock the Most Generous Generation

The aim of this book is to ensure your organization is empowered to be set up for the future of giving and generosity. To fully understand how to do this, you must understand the next generation of givers. One of the most important themes connected to the next generation of givers (millennials and Gen Z) is the incredible wealth transfer that is happening now and for the next few decades. Morgan Stanley reported it is the largest intergenerational wealth transfer in history, amounting to over $30 trillion in inheritance (OpenInvest, 2021)! In addition to that, millennial earning power will increase by 75% across the next few years.

The reason Morgan Stanley is studying and reporting on this is because it is a massive threat to their financial advisor business. A large portion of their assets under management (which determines a large portion of their compensation) will be transferred from their boomer clients to the next generations who don't necessarily need or want a financial advisor. This is a symptom of a larger sentiment with younger generations and how they want to manage their money overall.

SpendMeNot has a great list on how millennials manage money called "21 Massive Millennial Spending Stats" (Chapkanovska, 2022). I've linked this source in this chapter's references, but I will summarize it in my own words for you, speaking on behalf of millennials, as I am one.

1. We don't own homes.
2. We spend over $90,000 on rent before age 30.
3. We have multiple subscriptions for entertainment amounting to >$100 a month.
4. We spend more on coffee than on our retirement plans.
5. We are a sucker for Instagram ads.
6. We are also a sucker for overpriced cocktails.
7. We appreciate brands with values and will purchase from them.

8. We love style and spend a fashionable $524 on apparel every month.
9. Emergency funds are not important to us #Yolo.
10. At some point we've made a financial plan.
11. Our financial plan incorporates how much we spend online.
12. When we shop online, we specifically use Amazon, and it's a weekly ritual (or more!).
13. We love free delivery.
14. Surprisingly, millennial men are actually shopping more online than women.
15. Both men and women LOVE their skincare routines.
16. We don't own appreciating assets like houses, but rather, depreciating ones like cars.
17. We will spend money for our health care.
18. We absolutely love our pets and will spend a lot of money on them, more than our own health care.

However, despite being renters without a retirement, pet owners without a pension, and shoppers without savings, we still . . .
GIVE!
Leading to:

19. At least half of us millennials *give on a monthly basis to charity.*

Closing out with:

20. We will spend more than $4,000 annually on travel.
21. We have stocks! At least 66% of millennial investors do.

Over half of new investors in 2020 were born between 1981 and 1996.

The preference of asset classes are in the following order:

1. Stocks
2. Mutual funds
3. Cryptocurrencies

The key learnings for nonprofit organizations is that despite some of our questionable financial decisions, our generation wants to give. And this giving will increase as incomes continue to grow, and a multiplier effect will flow from the appreciation on investments that millennials will gain in time alongside the receipt of their inheritance.

A report from Deloitte predicts that by 2030, millennials will experience the fastest growth in net wealth out of any generation (Srinivas & Goradia, 2015).

Another *x* factor to all of the previous points is the potential of cryptocurrency growth with popular cryptocurrencies such as Bitcoin and Etherium (see Figure 2.1). In 2022, over 33.7 million US adults are said to own at least one cryptocurrency (Insider Intelligence, 2022), and 94% of cryptocurrency buyers are millennials and Gen Z (Gogol, 2022).

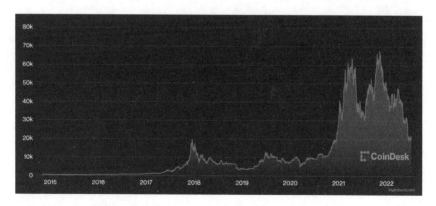

Figure 2.1   Bitcoin from 2015 to 2022

Source: Coindesk (n.d.).

What we can take away from the graph in Figure 2.1 is that although Bitcoin is significantly down from its peak, it is still significantly up from before its rise in 2017, which imputes a 50× return if you invested in that time. In context, Apple within that same time frame is up four times, and Amazon is up two times.

Regardless of your view of Bitcoin or the future of it, it's hard to deny the unprecedented appreciation it has experienced in the last five years. And even with the 2022 market downturn it seems to have a new price floor because of how many large institutions such as Block (formerly Square), Tesla, and Morgan Stanley have now backed it.

Here is why understanding the great wealth transfer and how future generations think about money management is so important. The average age of a donor in the United States is 64 (Double the Donation, 2022). This means most organizations are literally one generation away from not having access to the resources that they need to survive if they don't start appealing to the next generations. As boomers age out, they will transfer wealth (on the magnitude of $30 trillion) to millennials who are doing the following:

- Investing more
- Owning cryptocurrency
- Primarily transacting online through beautiful and easy-to-use e-commerce platforms

If you are not already appealing to this, you will miss out on the next generation of generosity.

Why Millennials Will Be the Most Generous Generation the World Has Ever Seen

Being in the Silicon Valley for the last decade has made me privy to the phenomena of angel investing. As I have seen my friends grow in their careers, increase in income, and do quite well with their stock compensation, more and more of them have participated in investing into early-stage start-up ventures, known as *angel investing*. Angel investing is a phenomenon that goes beyond portfolio management or even smart personal finance strategy. This is because of some seeming disadvantages:

- It is a very risky asset class (most start-up companies fail).
- It is very illiquid (it's difficult to exchange your shares in a start-up for cash).

If it's not smart financially and your money is locked in for years, why do people do it? I believe it is due to this key principle: status.

Angel investing has become a status symbol in Silicon Valley. The dream is to say you were one of the first checks into Uber or Airbnb. That your $25,000 pre-seed investment turned into millions because of your intelligence, intuition, and/or access.

The creation of platforms like AngelList have accelerated the popularity and participation in angel investing. In 2010, it wasn't cool to be an angel investor. Just a few years later, it started to become popularized and was the reason you got invited to certain parties in the San Francisco Bay Area. It's the topic of watercooler conversation. People started to put their AngelList profile on their Twitter bios, and it became an extension of their identity. Therefore, the acceleration of angel investing wasn't just a financial decision anymore. It was connected to who you are, what you believed your expertise was in, and what you believed in overall.

This phenomenon has extended into crypto and the Web3 community. There are tribes of those who believe solely in Bitcoin, or who speculate on meme coins like Dogecoin, or those who will spend thousands of dollars to have a "bored ape" as their profile picture on Twitter.

Where millennials spend or invest their money is influenced by what gives them social currency and represents what they believe their identity to be. The principle is not too different from previous generations. Although boomers might have found their identity, status, and social currency in their house, yard, and white picket fence, millennials and Gen Z find theirs in the matrix, avatars, and digital identities. No longer are the next generations fixated on bricks and mortar, but rather on bitcoin and the blockchain (we'll break down the blockchain and cryptocurrency in Chapter 4).

The ways millennials think about giving and generosity, in relation to identity, is the same. Check out this excerpt from a *Forbes* article written in 2019 (Bader, 2019):

Lazy, entitled, self-obsessed and uninvolved. These negative stereotypes often attributed to the millennial generation are now so well-known that they have become the shorthand by which we identify those born between the years 1981 and 1996.

However, a new survey conducted by Fidelity Charitable turns at least one assumption about millennials on its head. Millennials, it seems, are a very generous bunch. In fact, they give more than twice as much of their money and time to charitable causes as either baby boomers or Gen X.

Fidelity Charitable's survey of 3,000 adults, including 288 entrepreneurs, found that millennials, on average, donate $13,654 a year to charity, compared to $6,200 for Gen X and $6,192 for baby boomers.

There are also substantial differences in the way millennials give, according to the survey. For instance, they are more likely to value charitable giving opportunities that help them learn, grow, or expand their personal influence. They also see giving as part of their *core identity* and want to be more directly involved in how and where their donations are spent.

Generosity Is My Identity

There was a time where my wife Kim and I sold our house in order to give. It was 2018, and as a church I knew my pastor was preparing to announce a big vision element: we were going to go from five locations to ten locations, planting five more churches . . . in one year! Remember what I said in Chapter 1 . . . he's crazy. He has crazy faith and communicates bold vision!

In preparation for this particular vision gala, Kim and I were praying about the amount we wanted to give, a practice that we did every year the Monday before the Friday's vision gala. When we shared with each other what we both believed was in our heart to give, it was the same amount. This was incredible confirmation because we were aligned, and at the same time really confusing because we didn't have that agreed-on amount in the bank account. It was a very large amount for us at the time. Not wanting to show up on Friday with a fictitious number we could not follow through with, we started to think deeper about what we could do to have the means to give that amount.

After further prayer, we believed God highlighted our house as something we could sell so that we could give. At first, I thought that was the devil actually. Why would God compel us to sell our most treasured asset at the time? It was the only real form of asset ownership we had at that time. It was a coveted piece of property in the very expensive Bay Area!

Then I remembered this biblical principle: "where your treasure is, there your heart will also be." So maybe it wasn't the devil after all, and actually God compelling us to give.

As context, we had purchased this townhouse three years before scraping together all the savings we had and selling all of the Google employee shares I was granted early in my career to have enough of a down payment to get into the house. Thankfully, we bought at a decent time, and the real estate market in our city grew substantially in that time, which gave us a good amount of equity. Selling the house would give us more than enough to meet our giving goal and to be part of our church's vision that year to the level we aspired to! We wanted this equity that we had in our house, this equity that we treasured, to be aligned with where our heart wanted to go—which was being part of the vision for our church.

So we did it!

What would cause a couple like us to want to give at the level of selling their house in order to give?

Was it the vision that compelled us to sell our house? Partly! I believe the vision is imperative to inspire big giving. I would actually say that it is now table stakes if a donor is going to even consider giving at all. There needs to be a big vision paired with clear articulation of what the giving will unlock. Although this is an important component, I don't believe it's the primary reason someone would be willing to sell their house in order to give. Frankly, I've been inspired by bigger visions from other organizations, such as Charity: Water, bringing clean water to every human being on the planet, or New Story, who is 3D printing homes with the vision to end global homelessness. It would actually be really romantic for us to sell our home in order to build a home through New Story. The reality is that although we do support organizations such as this, we have never considered selling a major asset like our house in order to give to it.

Was it the delivery and presentation that compelled us to sell our house? The atmosphere, level of excellence for the event, importance of storytelling, and the level of conviction in your vision presentation all matter. The preparation and attention to detail communicate value, worth, and credibility.

It invites the donor to trust where their giving is going, and because you show that you care, they have an opportunity to care as well. Although I believe the delivery of the vision is critical, I would highlight that Kim and I decided to start the sales process of our house even before the fundraising gala event.

There are many other components I can list that are important and need to come together as a minimum standard to position your organization to raise big funds for a cause:

- Consistent communication throughout the year highlighting impact.
- Opportunities for givers to volunteer and see the impact of your organization up close and personal.
- Timing of giving campaigns being scheduled during natural waves of momentum, for example, end of year.

All of these are important, but not the primary reason a couple would sell their house in order to give.

Kim and I sold our house to give because *generosity had become our identity within the context of this community.*

For us it had become a core identity that didn't necessarily even need validation from others. There is no public list that is posted in our church that ranks the most generous people in the community. Although our church community is brilliant at recognition, there is no promise of status or public praise on the other side of a gift. What we had was an opportunity to act on something that was consistent with what we wanted to believe about ourselves.

When you see yourself as a generous person and have opportunities to reinforce that with your actions, you are willing to pursue that in extravagant ways. Through giving, we are deepening our identity in generosity, and that experience brings forth many benefits chemically to your brain. It's actually similar to why millennials have focused much of their spending on experiences. Because when you build meaningful memories through experiences by investing in things like travel, you don't only benefit from that during the life span of the trip but you also receive the similar levels of physiological reward every time you remember and recall the trip.

A focus on what we are able to do by giving can most definitely unlock significant giving. But speaking to who donors can become through their giving will unlock extravagant, over-the-top, sacrificial giving. We had an appetite to become a generous family because this is what was celebrated and modeled within our church. There is language for those that want to align themselves to this lifestyle of generosity, and in our church, it's called *kingdom builders*. Becoming a kingdom builder is a status that is to be aspired to, but one that doesn't necessarily need public recognition. It is motivated by simply knowing you have become one.

The most beautiful part of aspiring for this type of status is that it is not attached to pressure; rather, it is attached to privilege. It provides an opportunity for a person to become who they aspire to be. If I can reinforce who I am, more than what I do, it is the most purpose-driven state I can be in.

As organizations come to understand this, it will unlock a multitrillion-dollar opportunity with the next generation of giving. Fundraising events will not just be a place to get some donations done, but a celebration of generosity and what the community has become. The goal is to create and cultivate a community of givers who attach their identity to generosity. That's when big giving is unlocked and creativity is at its best. People start breaking off limitations of what's possible and give in new ways that maybe you wouldn't have even expected. Donors will have new energy in their careers and a reason for why they work so hard. It will not be for the sole purpose of earning a paycheck for themselves or to buy a bigger house but to be part of impact, meaning, change, and something beyond themselves. You know you have cultivated this type of community when you start receiving these types of gifts:

- The up-and-coming entrepreneurs in your community want to align their business value with your impact so they will give you a percentage of their revenues or equity in their company.
- The creatives—musicians and artists—in your community will want to distribute a percentage of royalties to your organization.
- Real estate investors will give from the equity appreciation in their properties to your organization.
- Collectors of art, wine, and sneakers will give from their capital gains in these assets to your organization.

In Chapter 3, I will explain what is happening technologically to make all these types of donations possible!

Why should you expect this type of exuberance for giving within your community? Because it's scientifically proven to be physiologically rewarding to the giver!

The Science of Generosity

Generosity and science don't seem like they belong in the same sentence. Can generosity be dissected in a lab? Is there a way to empirically measure how kind someone is? Is it just pseudoscience to believe generosity actually affects our well-being?

It may seem strange to look at giving, a more intrinsic idea, from a scientific lens. But recent research has proven that giving is great for our health on physical, emotional, and neurological levels.

Here are some of the noted benefits: stress reduction, improved mental health, longer lives, deeper emotional connection, and a general sense of feeling good.

Biologically, giving may seem counterintuitive. Aren't we supposedly bent toward survival and hoarding whatever resources possible? Aren't humans generally selfish?

On the contrary, science shows that we're wired to give. The saying "it's better to give than receive" isn't just a cute sentiment. We actually gain more when we give, which seems paradoxical.

A study done in 2015 found that performing daily acts of kindness lowered stress levels in participants. When they didn't practice generosity, their stress levels went up. That's because generosity increases levels of serotonin, dopamine, and oxytocin—chemicals in our body that help regulate mood and happiness (Scott, 2020).

One of the biggest strains on our mental health is anxiety, which is linked to stress. In another *New York Times* article published during the start of the pandemic, Wharton psychologist Adam Grant was quoted as saying, "There is a lot of evidence that one of the best anti-anxiety medications available is generosity" (Parker-Pope, 2020).

Hooked on a Feeling

Who doesn't want to feel good? Seemingly every part of our society is geared toward making us feel better, yet many of us are chronically unhappy.

In their groundbreaking book, *The Paradox of Generosity*, sociologists Christian Smith and Hillary Davidson (2014) researched, tracked, and interviewed individuals' spending habits over a five-year period. Here are some of their wild findings:

- 41% of Americans who donated 10% of their incomes said they never or hardly ever experienced depression.
- Those who described themselves as "very happy" volunteered almost six hours per month. Those who said they were "unhappy" volunteered just 0.6 hours.

- Those who were in giving relationships or practiced hospitality were more likely to be in "excellent health" than those who did not.

However, author Christian Smith emphasized that to reap the benefits of feeling good, generosity must be woven into our daily rhythms.

"It has to be a practice, it has to be something that is sustained over time, that people engage with regularly. One-off things just don't affect us that much, whereas things that we repeat, things that are sustained in our bodily behaviors and in our minds, have tremendous effects on us," he said in an interview with *The New Republic* (Smith, 2014).

Smith's findings make sense. As we just touched on, generosity has proven over and over to release feel good chemicals in our body. But we can't just do it to chase a high. It has to be an organic process; otherwise, we don't get the same benefits.

"You can't cynically try and look to get [an] effect," Smith said. "We have to learn just to be generous people."

Empathy Inside My DNA

In a recent *Scientific American* podcast, social psychologist Liz Dunn discussed an experiment in which people were given money to either keep for themselves or give to others. The results were somewhat surprising: "What we found, consistent with all our past research, was that the more money people gave away, the happier they felt. Conversely though, the more money people kept for themselves the more shame they experienced" (*Scientific American*, 2010).

Although giving isn't intended to only benefit us, it makes us feel good and builds connections with others. This warm glow effect, as it's called, "activates regions of the brain associated with pleasure, social connection, and trust," per an article from UC Berkeley (Suttie & Marsh, 2010). Giving also is linked to "less anxiety, less helplessness and hopelessness, better friendships and social networks."

In other words: it builds empathy and helps us to better understand perspectives of those around us.

Resting My Case on the Greatest Opportunity for Generosity This World Has Ever Seen

Millennials are inheriting wealth and are ready to put that to work. Where they will spend or give in big amounts will be the places that are connected to their identity. There are sociological, spiritual, and scientific dynamics driving this trend, and the best investment you can make is to understand these dynamics, hire the right people, and partner with the right technology platforms that will help you be best positioned to be a recipient of this wave of generosity that is already starting to crest.

Knowing everything you know now, after this chapter, you should ask the following questions about your organization:

- Do we communicate in a way that is compelling to millennials?
- Do we have any major gifts coming in from millennials today?
- What type of gifts are given from millennials today?
- Are we aligning our messaging to highlight both impact *and* identity?

Now that you know the keys to unlocking the most generous generation the world has ever seen, and how they will be creative with their generosity, Chapter 3 will dive into the actual cutting-edge technology becoming available to facilitate this next wave of giving!

3

The Evolution of Investable Asset Classes

Before we deep dive into specific noncash assets for donations, I would love to expose you to where financial technology is taking us. This will further highlight that the assets such as stocks and crypto that we will be talking about a lot in the next two chapters are simply just the beginning of a wave of investable assets that should be enabled to give.

In this chapter we will explore the hype of investable assets, the dangers that come with them, the corrections we have experienced through them, and how I believe the last few years have led us to a future with an acceleration of new investor entrants into the market. This group will continue to increase in their appetite for investing, but in an educated and strategic way.

As a nonprofit, your understanding of the potential future will open up your imagination for what's possible and also give you a vision for what giving could and should look like for your organization. I believe that as more people catch this vision, there will be more motivation to take the required steps to set you up for this future.

Being immersed in Silicon Valley since the early 2010s, I believe start-ups that are successful in high-growth fundraising are the ones that have a vision for the future before it exists in the present. That has reinforced a culture of innovation and being ahead of the curve in this region. I'd love this same mentality to be prevalent in the nonprofit fundraising space because I believe it will unlock exponential growth.

The Crypto Bull Run

Living through 2019–2021 taught me that the good ol' "get rich quick" scheme is alive and well. We saw peak activity and unprecedented bull runs across all investable asset classes—especially crypto—with a lot of credit going to the retail investor explosion during this time frame. This three-year run was crazy. Fear of missing out (FOMO) was at an all-time high. Every other hangout, Zoom call, and group chat had one of my friends or family members talking about the new cryptocurrency project they were invested into or how they were getting rich off of crypto. Sharing your portfolio, or rather, bragging about your portfolio, was the primary watercooler talk.

The problem with 90% of these cryptocurrency projects is that many people primarily got into them to "get rich." No one understood the underlying technology or even cared about the underlying mission of the project. It became so much hype that eventually we just all agreed out in the open what we were trying to do, so we called it meme coins. Literally, Doge coin started out as a meme—a joke. But with the hope of riches, people ran up the price by purchasing it at high levels, and the people who made money were the ones who planned their exit accordingly. This is called "pump and dump," in which inevitably someone is left holding the bag at the end of it.

A couple of examples of huge rises and falls in the crypto space include Terra Luna and Celcius. The collapse of the Terra network lost investors $40 billion dollars (Newbery, 2022). Celsius network, a titan in the crypto lending space, filed bankruptcy and was facing claims that it was running a Ponzi scheme by paying early depositors with the money it got from new users. After hitting a peak of $25 billion, it collapsed to sub $200 million and currently owes users about $4.7 billion (Sigalos, 2022). In both of these cases, the problem points either to pump-and-dump-like activity or the organization being overleveraged (borrowing too much against their actual assets). Or both.

There are many stories like this in the crypto space, and the common denominator is greed. The greedy will generate hype, and the hype will attract more greed, and the cycle continues until enough people realize that what they have put their money in has no real substance or utility. At its peak, crypto was at a $3 trillion market cap. At the time of writing this, it's lost two-thirds of that, as many cryptocurrencies are going to 0, or close to 0. Unfortunately, many regular people lost meaningful sums of money relative to what they have.

The good that can come from this is that the market learns from it and that there is a pursuit of education for investing and a reorientation in understanding the underlying value of an asset. Although the correction in crypto has been severe, it follows what is happening in the stock market as well, especially with high-growth technology stocks that may have been overvalued and lost any ties to fundamental business sense.

As a start-up founder, I saw this was the most egregious in the private markets. Hundreds of millions of dollars invested into founders, apps, ideas, and slide decks generating no revenue. Many actually hadn't even built a product yet. Nine- or ten-figure valuations pre-product has to be a sign of a frothy market that has lost sensibility. As the market violently corrected down in 2022, we saw many venture capitalists and investors overall reinstituting basic disciplines such as doing due diligence, paying attention to revenue multiples against public comparables, and reviewing important metrics such as growth rate, retention, and unit economics.

Although 2019–2021 brought into the market the most new retail investors history has ever seen (especially millennials and Gen Z), I believe 2022 and beyond will mark the point in which those investors don't depart, but instead become more educated. Investing is not going anywhere. Actually, retail investing and alternative investing has never been bigger.

For organizations that want to position themselves for high-growth fundraising, it's important to understand the trends emerging in the retail and alternative investing landscape so you position your organizations for the future.

Let's have some fun by taking a look at some emerging investing trends you may have not heard about powered by some breakthrough financial technology companies.

A High-Level View into Emerging Alternative Investing Trends

Masterworks' mission is to democratize the $1.7 trillion art market. Say what!? That's larger than the current crypto market at the time of writing this and formerly was a market that was restricted exclusively to the rich and famous. In 2017, the chief executive officer (CEO) Scott Lynn had a light bulb moment realizing that art is probably the largest asset class that's never been securitized. So how does it work?

1. Masterworks selects the artists, and their research team uses proprietary data to determine which artist markets have the most momentum.
2. Their acquisitions team locates what is believed to be a good piece and, at a fair price, purchases the work.
3. They securitize the artwork by filing an offering circular with the SEC and allowing anyone to invest.
4. They hold the artwork for three to ten years. Investors who bought shares in the artwork can wait until Masterworks sells the painting to receive pro rata proceeds, or they can sell shares on the secondary market.

Masterworks claims to be the largest art buyer in the world and is valued at over $1 billion as a company. The average investor on the platform invests $30,000. There is a lot of enthusiasm from investors, many of whom would have never had access to these art pieces if it wasn't for Masterworks, who touts that since 2000 blue-chip art has outperformed the S&P 500 by more than 250%. In 2019, the company acquired Banksy's iconic *Mona Lisa* and IPO'd it to its members for $1,030,000. In just one year, Masterworks sold the artwork for $1,500,000, netting investors an annualized return of 32%.

Rally is another platform that is fractionalizing ownership for alternative assets but is diversified across multiple collectibles beyond art (see Figures 3.1, 3.2, and 3.3). Think cars, sports memorabilia, books, cards, comics, and most recently, NFTs. The process of how it works is very similar to Masterworks, but unlike Masterworks, Rally does not charge any commissions or management fees on the value of user investments. Although Masterworks is democratizing investments typically only available to the ultra-rich, Rally seems to be

Figure 3.1 Star wars action figure worth $18,000

Source: Rally / RSE Markets, https://rallyrd.com/collections/, last accessed Oct 05, 2022.

Figure 3.2 Signed game basketball worth $105,000

Source: Rally / RSE Markets, https://rallyrd.com/collections/, last accessed Oct 05, 2022.

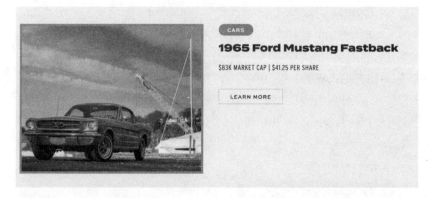

Figure 3.3   Classic Ford Mustang worth $83,000

Source: Rally / RSE Markets, https://rallyrd.com/collections/, last accessed Oct 05, 2022.

focused on making pop culture investable. They have a really cool edge about them. I had an opportunity to meet some of the founders and visit their retail storefront right in the heart of Soho in New York City which serves as more of a branding play and a place to display some of their collectibles. Rally is definitely one of the emerging fintech apps that is making investing cool.

Vinovest is another platform that has been growing fast. If Rally is making investing cool, then Vinovest is making investing classy. The founder, Anthony Zhang, writes comprehensive tweet threads of the history and back stories of different wines and has become a great evangelist for how fine wine has been the best-kept secret in investing, until they came along. The benefits of wine investing include the following:

- **Inflation-resistant:** Although inflation can make your groceries, gas, and rent more expensive, it has little effect on fine wine, which makes it a perfect hedge against rising prices.

- **Recession-resistant:** Vinovest highlights that during COVID-19, while the Dow and S&P 500 plummeted −22.7% and −19.6%, respectively, fine wine only fell −1.4%.
- **Low volatility:** Fine wine has had consistent performance even when the stock market takes major swings up and down.
- **Tax advantages:** Vinovest has bonded warehouses that don't charge an excise and value-added tax (VAT).
- **Diversification:** This is a main sticking point for Vinovest. Although stocks, bonds, and mutual funds are all vulnerable to similar factors, fine wine has low correlation with those factors, which makes it a great diversification tool.

One of my favorite differentiators of Vinovest is that you actually own the wine. You can buy, sell, or even drink it if you choose. Following are some factors that drive the value of wine:

- **Scarcity:** Wineries often make investment-grade wines in limited quantities—a few hundred bottles or so. That number falls as people drink them.
- **Aging:** Wine improves with time.
- **Brand equity:** Screaming Eagle or Domaine de la Romanée-Conti rank among the most prestigious names in wine and command six-figure prices per bottle.

AngelList is one of the pioneers into democratizing and popularizing investing into start-up companies. In their 2021 year-in-review, they list some of the following accomplishments:

- $3.6 billion invested into funds and syndicates on the platform
- 800+ VCs running their funds on the platform
- 11,000+ investments made by VCs on AngelList

- $22 million saved for founder in legal and admin fees versus the traditional route

With more than 15,000 funds and syndicates now on the platform, I have personally experienced the proliferation of AngelList with many of my friends who invest through it, founders accessing capital with it, and VCs using it to execute on deals. Many investors are looking for the next Uber, Airbnb, or DoorDash deal, and if they are lucky they might find it on AngelList. In fact, 190 unicorns have been backed by AngelList funds and syndicates with more than 12,000 total start-ups funded, and counting! With technology investments continuing to be made in this space with other players such as Carta, the cap table management software, and continued demand for these assets, you can imagine a world where shares in certain private start-up companies will be as liquid as public market securities.

Real estate. Don't forget the largest asset class of them all, which represents the biggest driver of wealth globally: real estate. Over the last 200 years, 90% of the world's millionaires have been created by investing in real estate (Yates, 2021). Because homeownership remains the main driver of wealth, especially for the bottom 50%, new fintech entrants such as Fundrise are adamant about democratizing that further.

Real estate is the most important alternative investment asset class for the bottom 50% based on net worth, while equities and stocks are the most important for the top 1% (see Figure 3.4).

Fundrise is a real estate investing platform that offers a low-cost, diversified portfolio of institutional-quality real estate. Their strategy is specifically a value-investing strategy that acquires assets for less than what they believe is their intrinsic value, and typically less than their replacement cost. Since 2012, they've invested more than $4 billion worth of real estate across the US and manage more than $1 billion of equity across 300,000 individual investors.

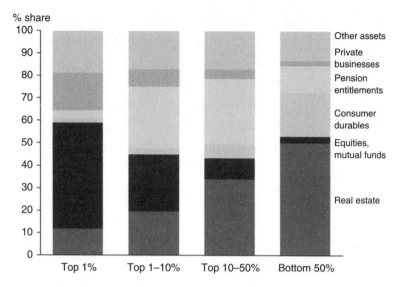

Figure 3.4 Type of portfolio assets across wealth distribution

Source: Board of Governors of the Federal Reserve System (2021).

What the Growth of Alternative Investing Means for the Nonprofit Fundraiser

Why did I take you on this tour of alternative investment products? Because I believe every nonprofit fundraiser should know about the trends in financial technology and investing that are responsible for the greatest net new entrants in the investing market that the world has ever seen. Alternative investing has surpassed $10 trillion in 2020, which is about a quarter of the public securities market, and I believe it will continue to accelerate. Where there is wealth generation, there is opportunity for people to give!

The more that assets are being securitized, the more assets should be able to be given . . . easily. If more assets are being digitized and fractionalized so that you can own shares in a collectible, car, bottle of wine, or an art piece, then you should be able to give it without friction. This is where the world of giving is going, and your organization needs to be ready to receive it.

Now that we have done a robust tour on the longer tail of alternative investments, let's do a deep dive on the most important noncash asset investments in regards to giving. Chapters 4 and 5 will deep dive specifically into crypto and stock donations.

4 | Deep Dive into Cryptocurrency

Without going into great detail, cryptocurrency is a decentralized digital asset. Anyone around the world can make a crypto transaction by buying crypto with fiat currency, selling crypto for fiat currency, or trading crypto. Transactions are recorded on a blockchain, which is a distributed ledger that is run by a network of computers—meaning it is not owned by a single entity or regulated by the US government. Because cryptocurrency is encrypted by nature, it is nearly impossible to hack, manipulate, or double-spend, making it a trustworthy form of currency.

Cryptocurrency, also known as crypto, is a digital form of currency. Over the past several years, crypto has slowly integrated into the mainstream economy and has become an accepted form of payment by major retailers like Starbucks and Home Depot. In 2020 to 2021 there was a huge spike in crypto investors and enthusiasts who have recognized the value of cryptocurrency as an alternative investment option. Like stock, crypto investors can buy, sell, trade, and use crypto as an investment vehicle for short-term and long-term capital gains. The information in this chapter is going to be vital to your knowledge as a high-growth fundraiser as we dive deep into the what, who, and how of crypto investing and donations.

How Does Crypto Gain Value?

One of the best ways to understand how crypto gains value is comparing Bitcoin to gold.

Gold is a precious metal that is highly valued globally, yet there is a finite amount of it. Because of gold's limited supply and high demand, the value of gold is fairly high. That value is also determined by how much interest people have in owning it.

Similar to gold, some cryptocurrency value is affected by supply and demand. For instance, some cryptocurrencies only have a limited number of coins available for sale. As more coins are mined (brought into circulation) and distributed to crypto investors, there are fewer coins that remain unmined, capping future supply. The dwindling supply (paired with the recent surge in societal interest) has continued to increase the value of certain cryptocurrencies over the past few years, resulting in significant appreciation for early investors.

Unlike gold, which is *one* specific precious metal, cryptocurrency represents *multiple* digital currencies. Popular cryptocurrencies include Bitcoin, Binance Coin, and Ethereum (Ether), among many more. There is a maximum number of coins made for certain cryptocurrencies (e.g., Bitcoin), and the demand of those limited supply cryptocurrencies indicates the value of it. So, for example, when there is discussion about the price of Bitcoin versus Ethereum (Ether), those are two separate digital currencies with separate monetary values attached. This is important to understand because if a donor expresses interest in donating "cryptocurrency", you should know that there is a delineation between different coins and projects.

Who Are Crypto Investors?

Literally anyone can be a crypto investor—all you need is a bank account or credit card and access to the internet. Although anyone can invest in crypto, we are seeing trends in the profile of a typical crypto investor.

The Crypto Investor Persona

- 14% of Americans own crypto, which translates to roughly 21.2 million Americans.
- 74% of men versus 24% of women are crypto owners.
- 77% of crypto owners are under 45 years old, the average age being 38 years old.
- 71% of crypto owners are White, followed by 13% Hispanic/Latino/Mexican, 10% Asian American/Pacific Islanders, and 9% African American/Black (Gemini, 2022).

Crypto investors tend to be in the younger millennial generation (ages 25 to 40). Typical crypto investors are tech-savvy and excited by crypto's innovation. They view the decentralized nature of crypto as economic democracy and are unafraid of the crypto market's volatility because they see huge profit potential.

One of the more interesting facets of millennials is their level of engagement in organizations they truly want to support. Highly educated, civic-minded, and driven to make an impact in the world, this demographic is more inclined to charitable giving and volunteering (Hoss, 2021). About 75% of millennials consider themselves philanthropists, and nine in ten say charitable giving is of major importance in their lives (Fidelity Charitable, 2021). Additionally, according to *The Millennial Impact Report*, 90% of millennials said they stop giving to organizations when they distrust the organization. Another 90% said they are motivated to give by a compelling mission (Hoss, 2021). This is great news for nonprofits. If nonprofits leverage millennials as a donor group from a mission-driven standpoint (coupled with the option to give crypto), there could be a significant impact in this digital funding stream.

Accepting Crypto Donations for Your Nonprofit

Now that you know the "what" and the "who", let's dive deeper into the trends and the practicalities of how to best accept crypto donations for your organization.

Trends in Crypto Giving

Data have proven that crypto investors are disproportionately generous compared to other investor communities. Of Fidelity Charitable's full investor population, 45% of crypto investors donated $1,000 or more, while only 33% of the general investor population donated that same amount to charity in 2020. Overall, $158 million in crypto assets were donated at Fidelity Charitable in 2021, which was a 464% increase from 2020 (Fidelity Charitable, 2021).

Additionally, the number of crypto owners is rising. In 2021, crypto owners increased from 106 million (January 2021) to 221 million (June 2021) to 296 million (December 2021). It's estimated that soon, there will be *1 billion crypto owners globally* (Crypto.com, 2022). Domestically, about 14% of the US population (that's over 20 million American adults) have said they are invested in crypto, and approximately 19.3 million American adults plan to purchase crypto within 2022 (Gemini, 2022). High crypto adoption rates coupled with the influx in crypto donations makes this new digital currency hard to ignore.

Why Are Crypto Investors Donating?

For millennials, using cryptocurrency as an investment asset *and* giving back to charity is important, but the big question is *why* are they donating?

There are several reasons why millennial crypto owners are donating:

- They're an idealistic, younger generation wanting to donate to causes they believe in.
- Millennial crypto investors now have appreciated crypto investments as available capital to be given away. Depending on when an investor started investing in crypto, there still may be significant appreciated gains even through the 2022 crypto market correction.
- The COVID-19 pandemic accelerated attention of millennials to donate to health and human service nonprofits as well as other nonprofits affected by the crisis. In addition to intrinsic rewards, *one significant reason as to why crypto investors are donating: tax benefits.*

Cryptocurrency sold or exchanged for profit is subject to capital gains tax (and, in some cases, state income tax). When a crypto investor sells or exchanges their crypto profit for cash, then the length of time they held their crypto indicates their capital gains tax burden. If they held it for less than a year, then short-term capital gains tax applies (up to 37%), but if it's longer than a year, long-term capital gains tax applies (up to 20%).

However, tax-savvy crypto investors can avoid this and receive a tax deduction by donating their crypto. *When crypto is donated directly to a nonprofit, donors can avoid paying capital gains tax on appreciated crypto, and they receive a federal income tax deduction.* The length of time the crypto was held will determine the federal income tax deduction. As of the date of donation, crypto that is held short term (less than a year) will receive a deduction for the original amount paid for the crypto (basis). Crypto held long term (longer than a year) will receive a federal income tax deduction for the fair market value of the crypto. Donors could always sell their crypto for cash and then donate the cash, but this would be disadvantageous because the donor would have to pay capital gains tax. This would result in an ultimately smaller donation.

The Top Five Exciting Things About Crypto Donations for Nonprofits

With a clearer understanding of cryptocurrency, who crypto investors are, and its global growth, we can get excited about what this means for nonprofits.

- **A net new pool of donors.**
  - Traditionally, the typical donor is 64 years old, they donate twice a year, and they aren't donating crypto (Double the Donation, 2022). When nonprofits integrate crypto donations into their fundraising strategies, they are opening themselves

to a whole new pool of donors in the millennial and Gen Z generations. Millennials currently outnumber baby boomers, and they are adopting and donating crypto at a rapid rate. By tapping into this age group and cryptocurrency, nonprofits could see gifts increase by the hundreds of thousands.

- **Tax efficiencies.**
  - Donating crypto is a win–win for donors and nonprofits. When donors donate crypto to a 501(c)3 tax exempt nonprofit, then the donation is tax deductible. Depending on how long the crypto was held, donors will be able to deduct either the basis value or the fair market value of the crypto donation. They'll also avoid paying capital gains tax on the appreciated crypto. When nonprofits receive a crypto donation directly, they receive the full market value of the crypto at the time of donation. This could have been up to 37% less if the donor sold the crypto and donated the cash. Thus, the donor can make a larger gift leveraging the tax benefits of donating an appreciated capital asset directly to a nonprofit.
- **Larger gifts.**
  - When we said crypto donors are disproportionately generous, we meant it. As of 2021, the average online cash donation was $128 versus the average crypto donation of $10,455 (The Giving Block, 2021). Nonprofits that integrate crypto acceptance tools often see 82× larger donations than online cash donations from their existing and prospective donors.
- **Crypto giving is only going up.**
  - As crypto enthusiasm continues to surge globally, it's projected that well over 40 million Americans will own crypto by 2023. It's obvious that crypto investment has become a strategic, diversified financial move by the average American. As crypto investors see their digital assets become a more important part of their holdings, they'll look for ways to make an impact and give back, opening a completely new revenue stream for nonprofits.

- **We can make accepting crypto easy.**
  - By partnering with platforms such as Overflow.co, we can implement a seamless crypto donation experience for donors. By integrating technology, donors can come to the nonprofit's website and donate crypto within minutes. These platforms provide the nonprofit with back-office tools for accounting purposes, saving time and logistical headaches. The automation also ensures donors and nonprofits are IRS compliant.

Launching, Fundraising, and Scaling with Crypto Donations

Cryptocurrency is not a passing fad. In 2021 alone, the crypto market and mainstream adoption of it exploded. Some major crypto advances in 2021: Crypto's value hit $3 trillion in assets with 14% of the US population invested; El Salvador announced it would make Bitcoin legal tender; the first crypto company, Coinbase, went public valuing at $85.8 billion; and the first Bitcoin ETF launched, allowing investors to invest in the ETF without actually trading Bitcoin. Since then, the crypto space continues to experience volatility, but the 2021 peaks and milestones indicates its potential.

Crypto has proven to be a growing source of capital, and it's time for the nonprofit space to get in on the action. As we know, crypto donors are more inclined to give more than non-crypto donors. We can now give donors the opportunity to donate crypto by implementing a seamless, innovative donor experience. But first, it's important to give nonprofits the tools they need to be successful in crypto philanthropy.

The following steps will give you everything you need to know about successfully accepting crypto donations at your nonprofit:

1. Internal education for receiving crypto donations
2. A modern and self-service crypto donation channel

3. Placement of crypto giving options
4. Consistency across platforms elevates awareness
5. Donor awareness and education
6. Generating donor enthusiasm

Step 1: Internal Education for Receiving Crypto Donations

Accepting crypto donations may sound intimidating, but it doesn't have to be daunting. It's just a matter of educating your gift officers and marketing team on what cryptocurrency is, how it can be advantageous as a gifting opportunity (i.e., tax benefits), and how to donate crypto.

Gifting officers, the marketing team, and potentially everyone within the organization should be able to explain the basics of donating crypto to donors.

Simply put:

1. **Donate.** A donor visits your organization's website and selects the cryptocurrency (e.g., Bitcoin, Ethereum, etc.) and how much they want to donate.
2. **Transfer.** Within minutes, the crypto is transferred from the donor to the nonprofit and is liquidated at the market value of the crypto.
3. **Receive.** The donor will receive a tax receipt reflecting the donation amount they can use as charitable deduction on income tax filings. And the nonprofit receives the net cash from the liquidated asset.

In addition to understanding the basics of crypto donations, the marketing team within your organization has to be well-versed in speaking to the new demographic of donors: millennials. It's vital to understand that crypto donors are most likely young professionals, tech-savvy, civic-oriented, living in urban US regions, and women and men with diverse ethnic backgrounds. Additionally, your marketing team will need to know exactly how this demographic prefers to be communicated with (e.g., social media, text messages, via influencers) as a way to optimize marketing budgets and efforts.

It's also important to note that the IRS views crypto donations as gifted property. Officers at your nonprofit and donors will be responsible to file appropriately with the IRS.

- **Accepting crypto *directly* and liquidating within three years.** The nonprofit will file Form 8282 with the IRS and send a copy to the donor. Additionally, nonprofits will have to include crypto donations as a noncash contribution on Schedule M (Form 990).
- **Accepting crypto donations over $250.** The nonprofit must provide the donor with a contemporaneous written acknowledgment of the donation.
- **Accepting crypto donations over $5,000.** The nonprofit may be asked by the donor to sign Part IV of Form 8283, which acknowledges receipt of the property. Additionally, the donor will most likely need an independent appraisal of the donated crypto for filing purposes.

Step 2: A Modern and Self-Service Crypto Donation Channel

More and more nonprofits are looking to expand donor pools and diversify sources of funding. Accepting crypto donations accomplishes both. To do that, your nonprofit needs to implement simple, modern, self-service crypto donation technology that makes donating crypto as easy as venmo or cash app on their mobile phone.

A modern, self-service donation flow should look like this:

1. Crypto donation technology is implemented and enabled on the nonprofit's website.
2. The donor accesses the nonprofit's website and selects the donate crypto option.
3. The donor selects the cryptocurrency and amount of crypto they would like to give.
4. The nonprofit's QR code is displayed and ready to scan.
5. The donor opens their digital wallet and scans the QR code.
6. The crypto is transferred and liquidated within minutes, which retains the market value of the crypto for the nonprofit and the donor.
7. The donor receives a tax receipt and/or acknowledgment letter for income tax filing purposes

Implementing a digital crypto giving solution on your organization's website creates a seamless giving experience for donors as well as a back-office automated processes that reduces reporting and processing hours, decreases human error, and saves your staff's time to focus on other fundraising initiatives that push your nonprofit's mission forward. The best way to do this is to simply partner with a technology platform like Overflow that has already built the frontend and back-office tooling to enable this for your organization. Attempting to try and build it yourself will be a fool's errand because it will cost a lot of money and will not benefit from the learnings across hundreds of organizations on the platform. Platforms like Overflow have teams that can collaborate with your IT or website admin to easily install the giving solution on your website as well as train key staff on how to manage the giving on the backend.

Step 3: Placement of Crypto Giving Options

One key factor to succeeding with crypto fundraising is to ensure the crypto giving option is *placed prominently* alongside any other cash, credit, or stock giving buttons on the website. The millennial demographic, most likely to donate crypto, will abandon the donating process if the website or technology takes too long to use. Make the crypto giving option obvious with minimal clicks to maximize crypto giving.

Tips to focus on for successful placement and donation flow:

- **Prominence**
  - Reduce the number of clicks it takes to arrive at the "Give Crypto" button.
  - Add a "Give Crypto" option to the nonprofit's homepage, "Other Ways to Give" page, the main "Donations" page, and create a dedicated "Donating Crypto" landing page to the site.
- **Clear language**
  - Place very specifically labeled buttons and links on the non-profit's website that say, "Give Crypto" or "Donate Crypto."
- **Education and awareness in the giving flow**
  - Giving crypto is a new concept for many long-term donors and first-time donors. Add a message such as "Maximize the impact of your donation and increase your tax savings by donating crypto directly" to educate or reiterate the tax benefits to donating crypto.

Step 4: Consistency Across Platforms Elevates Awareness

With the right placement of crypto giving options, nonprofits can generate hundreds of thousands of dollars in crypto giving, triggering a new funding stream from existing and new donors. However, having a crypto giving button on your nonprofit's website doesn't do much unless you have consistency through an omni-channel (or multichannel) messaging and marketing strategy across applicable platforms.

Here's some useful advice in building awareness across platforms that millennials use:

Social Media

- Build crypto giving into the social media calendar to announce and promote crypto giving.
- Create organic and paid content for social media platforms that spread the message of the nonprofit's mission, how to donate crypto, and the tax benefits of donating crypto. Use social media platforms like TikTok, Instagram, YouTube, Twitter, Snapchat, Reddit, and LinkedIn.
- During major events use relevant hashtags in social media posts like #GivingTuesday, #BitcoinTuesday, and #Crypto-GivingTuesday.
- Engage with social media influencers who have a genuine interest and are enthusiastic about the nonprofit's mission.
- Monitor, share, and engage with social media posts when the nonprofit is tagged—especially by micro and macro influencers.
- When making a fundraising request to followers, explicitly include crypto giving as an option and highlight the tax savings from donating crypto.
- Include a direct crypto giving link in the nonprofit's social media bios or "About Us" section.

Mobile

- Use SMS marketing to alert donors of trends and events such as #GivingTuesday and #BitcoinTuesday or when the crypto market is spiking.

- Inform existing donors via mobile text that crypto giving is available on the nonprofit's website with a link to the crypto giving landing page.

Email

- Any time a nonprofit includes an ask in an email or has a link to donate, make sure that link leads directly to a giving page that includes a crypto donation option.
- Include subject lines and taglines such as "Maximize your impact with crypto donations."
- Increase communications when the crypto market spikes.
- Incorporate a link in the nonprofit's employee email signatures that the nonprofit is now accepting crypto, with a link to the crypto giving landing page.

Events

- Include a way for donors to buy tickets using crypto donations.
- Highlight crypto giving as an option on the "Call to Action" giving slide.
- Add a QR code on posters, fliers, and slides with a direct link to crypto donations.
- Post photos and videos related to crypto gifting on social media at the event in real time via stories, lives, retweets, and so on.

Content Pieces

- Create a robust content strategy with content that can be searched on Google. Millennials want to search and find informative videos, blog posts, e-books, whitepapers, case studies, and donor stories and testimonials. On each content piece, circle back to the nonprofit's mission as well as offer a value proposition, such as the tax benefits of donating crypto.

- Add a link or QR code that links to your crypto giving landing page on each printed content piece, such as brochures, fliers, schedules, announcements, and so on.

Platforms Not to Use

- Traditional outbound marketing methods will not be effective with millennials. Millennials resonate with what they feel is authentic content discovered on their own versus company-focused, impersonal content that is thrown at them. Avoid the following platforms when marketing to millennials:

  - **Phone.** They won't answer.
  - **Direct mail.** They'll throw it out.
  - **Radio advertising.** They either have a paid streaming service for music or do not listen to the radio.
  - **Magazine ads.** Nearly 100% of millennials use the internet and nine out of ten have a smartphone (Moraes, 2020)—they do not read print material.

Step 5: Donor Awareness and Education

The biggest barrier to receiving crypto donations is the lack of awareness that nonprofits have the technology and proper processes to accept crypto. Additionally, most existing and prospective donors aren't aware that crypto giving is the most tax-efficient way to give back.

The best thing a nonprofit can do is educate, engage, and repeat when it comes to informing donors about crypto giving.

- **Educate** your current donor pool and potential new donors on the *tax efficiency* of donating crypto. Emphasize how *easy it is to donate crypto* through the nonprofit's website and how donating crypto will *maximize impact*. This is a win–win for donors, who receive significant tax savings, and nonprofits, which receive a larger contribution than if the donor sold crypto and donated the cash.

- **Engage** with your crypto donors. Whether they are posting about donating to nonprofits, asking questions about crypto donations, or are interested in the impact of crypto donations—be available to respond, engage, educate, and show appreciation for gifts through social media posts and other content pieces.

- **Repeat** the benefits of donating crypto. Through multiple marketing platforms, someone must listen to, see, and hear a message at least seven times for the message to sink in. By repeatedly educating and engaging with donors about crypto giving, it will expand the donor pool, tap into a new, noncash asset fundraising channel, and increase the average size of gifts to the organization.

There's a small percentage of existing and prospective donors who truly understand the tax benefits in a way that drives consistent crypto donations. Therefore it's crucial for nonprofits to provide high-level education on the potential tax benefits and highlight that crypto is the most tax-efficient way to give. However it's also important to encourage donors to be intentional in evaluating the overall tax impact of their charitable giving plan with a CPA or wealth manager. (*This book and Overflow are not meant to be taken as tax advice. Please consult a tax professional for information about any potential tax implications associated with charitable giving.*)

Step 6: Generating Donor Enthusiasm

Now that you know the benefits of donating crypto and the huge impact crypto gifts can make toward a nonprofit's mission, it's important to generate enthusiasm in the crypto donor community. Following are some messaging options a nonprofit can begin to incorporate on its websites, emails, social media posts, and any other pieces of marketing collateral:

Save more on taxes by gifting crypto.

Donate crypto. Change lives.

Increase your gift by up to 37% by donating crypto! Instead of selling crypto to donate cash, you can now select the crypto you want to give and donate it directly to [nonprofit name]. Visit [nonprofit website] and donate today!

Make a big impact. Donate Bitcoin and other crypto to [nonprofit]. You can now donate up to 37% more with a direct crypto donation than if you sold your crypto and donated cash.

Did you know you can donate your crypto to [nonprofit]?

We now accept Bitcoin and other cryptocurrencies. By donating crypto you'll make a larger impact on [nonprofit mission] and as an added bonus, you'll save on taxes because of your charitable donation. Visit [nonprofit website] and learn more today.

Impact/support [nonprofit mission] and get a tax benefit through crypto donations. Donate crypto to [nonprofit] now.

Tax-savvy donors are now putting their crypto investments to good use by donating to charity. Donate Bitcoin or the crypto of your choice to [nonprofit] to make an impact on [nonprofit mission] and receive a tax deduction.

Maximize your charitable donations by donating crypto! We now accept Bitcoin and other cryptocurrencies directly. Visit [nonprofit website] and donate crypto without having to sell your crypto.

We are now accepting Bitcoin and other crypto! Visit [nonprofit website] and select donate crypto. Donate however much you like and receive a tax receipt. Your donation will be sold for cash and immediately used for [nonprofit mission]!

Now it's even easier to be generous. We are now accepting cryptocurrency. Just visit [nonprofit website] and select the crypto you'd like to donate. Within minutes your crypto is transferred and sold. You'll receive a receipt for a tax deduction, and we'll receive the cash your crypto was sold for. Your donation will immediately be put toward furthering [nonprofit mission].

You can donate more than cash to [nonprofit]. We are now accepting crypto. Visit us today and donate the crypto of your choice. Your crypto donation will be used to support [nonprofit mission]. In addition to your generosity, you'll be able to file for a tax deduction for the value of your crypto donation. Get started today at [nonprofit website].

Now that we have completed our deep dive into crypto donations, we will do the same for stock donations, which represents an even bigger immediate opportunity for your organization. While the cryptocurrency market cap is between $1 to $3 trillion today, the public securities and stock market is valued at over $40 trillion!

5

Deep Dive into Stock Donations

Charitable organizations have successfully focused fundraising efforts on cash giving for decades. Their loyal and passionate donors have followed suit with 80% of charitable donations coming in the form of cash (Axelrad, 2018).

But it's time to start *reimagining the future of philanthropy*. Although 80% of charitable donations are made in cash, or from donors' checking and savings account, US households hold only 10% of their overall wealth in these accounts (Axelrad, 2018). The periodic run-ups in the US stock market, the democratization of retail stock trading and the increase in capital gain tax rates have donors evaluating new ways to give.

The nonprofit organizations that adopt and pioneer stock donations will be best positioned to tap into the most underused fundraising asset. Nonprofits should be empowered to develop new processes and strategies to capitalize on stock giving to supplement their existing cash fundraising efforts. To maximize the potential, it is critical to understand the macro-level dynamics driving the necessary shift to noncash fundraising.

What Is Driving the Need to Support Stock Donations at Scale?

There are two primary drivers prompting nonprofits to focus on capturing the next generation of charitable giving:

- Significant donor wealth is held in liquid noncash assets, including stocks.
- Stock giving is the most tax-efficient way for donors to express generosity.

Noncash Assets Are the Next Donation Channel for Donors

Cash makes up less than 10% of the collective assets owned by Americans, which means nonprofits that solicit only cash gifts will be ignoring 90% of the total potential donation value. Stock has been and will continue to be an attractive investment asset for donors. Research has shown that 80% of affluent and high-net-worth individuals own appreciated assets, such as stocks, mutual funds, or bonds, but *only 19% of those donors have contributed these types of assets to charity* (Fidelity Charitable, 2016).

The Federal Reserve conducted a recent study that highlights the increase to 41.5% in the value of stocks held as a percentage of financial assets by US households, which represents a 70-year high (see Figure 5.1). (Other than stocks, financial assets also include bonds, cash, certificates of deposit, and bank deposits.)

The race to move wealth into the stock market is evident in the increasing number of brokerage accounts in the United States. In 2020, individual investors opened more than 10 million new brokerage accounts, which is an all-time record for a single year. The United States now sits with more than 100 million brokerage accounts and users, which represents an 11% increase from 2019.

Percent of directly and indirectly held corporate equities

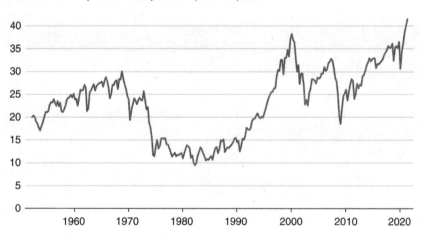

Source: Board of Governors of the Federal Reserve System (US), Households and Nonprofit Organizations; retrieved from FRED, Federal Reserve Bank of St. Louis

Figure 5.1   Household financial assets breakdown

Source: Board of Governors of the Federal Reserve System (US) (n.d.).

The Top Brokerages by Accounts Opened

- Fidelity: 32.5 million accounts
- Vanguard: 30 million users
- Schwab: 29.6 million accounts
- Webull: 15 million users
- Robinhood: 13 million users
- Interactive Brokers: 1.1 million accounts

The demographic trends also support the noncash asset ownership trend for the next generation of giving (see Figure 5.2). Gen Z and millennials are expanding the types of assets in which they hold wealth. App downloads for brokerage firms, popular with these two demographic segments, are also seeing record levels, with the Robinhood Markets Inc. app reaching 3.29 million downloads in January 2021 alone (Statista, 2021).

Given the buy and hold nature of stock investments, donors' overall wealth held in stock generally increases over time. Between 2000 and 2019, the average annualized return of the S&P 500 Index

Which of the following types of investments do you own?			
	Gen Z (aged 18 to 24)	Millennials (aged 25 to 40)	All investors aged 18 to 40
Stocks	73%	66%	67%
Mutual funds	35%	47%	45%
Cryptocurrency	47%	39%	40%
Bonds	30%	35%	34%
Stock options	39%	30%	31%
Index funds	22%	25%	24%

Figure 5.2   Millennial and Gen Z investment holdings

Source: Jack Caporal (2021) / The Motley Fool.

was 8.87% (Anspach, 2022). After the initial purchase of stock, the appreciation over time creates capital gains that are taxed when the investor eventually sells the stock. But what happens if a donor with equity investments wants to give that appreciated stock to a nonprofit organization?

Stock Giving Is the Most Tax-Efficient Way to Give

US tax law generally categorizes stock held for investment as a *capital asset*. When an investor purchases a capital asset, including stock, the amount paid creates the *cost basis* for the investment. If the *fair market value* of the stock increases over time, the difference between the fair market value and the original cost basis, known as a *capital gain*, will be taxed when the stock is eventually sold.

There is magic to be made when donating appreciated stocks to nonprofit organizations. And tax-savvy donors are looking to the nonprofits they support to create a seamless fundraising channel to donate stock.

When donors give appreciated stock, the shares are transferred from the donors' brokerage account directly to the nonprofit's brokerage account. If the receiving organization is a qualified 501(c)3 charitable organization and the donor has held the stock for more than one year, *the donor does not have to pay tax on the capital gain*. In addition, the full value (or fair market value) of the donated stock is the amount of the charitable donation donors can claim on their individual income tax returns.

This is a huge win–win for both the donor and the nonprofit. *In most cases, donors should not sell appreciated stock held over one year, pay capital gains tax, and then donate the remaining after-tax cash.*

Supporting stock donations empowers donors to make larger gifts to nonprofits while also reducing their personal taxes. This is the outcome the US government has encouraged and why there is an incentive in the tax code for charitable stock giving.

	Liquidate Then Donate	Donate Direct
Cost Basis of Stock	$5,000	$5,000
Fair Market Value	$10,000	$10,000
Capital Gains Tax %	20%	-
Capital Gains Tax	($1,000)	-
Total Donation	$9,000	$10,000

Figure 5.3   Appreciated stock donation example

Let's walk through the quick example shown in Figure 5.3 to highlight the benefits for a donor who plans to donate stock with $5,000 in appreciated value. If the donor sold the stock prior to donating it to the nonprofit, the donation would be $1,000 less (based on a 20% capital gain tax rate) than the fair market value today. By donating the stock directly, donors can give more to the nonprofits they care about.

So stock donations are the hot fundraising topic, but does stock giving translate to success for nonprofit organizations that do accept stock donations?

Stock Donations Fuel Nonprofit Fundraising

Nonprofits that receive stock donations see 55% higher fundraising growth than those that accept only cash (Russell, n.d.). Stock gifts tend to be larger than traditional donations, so the charities that accept stock donations often see a significant increase in their total giving within three months—without having to attract new donors (see Figure 5.4).

Russell James published a study after reviewing more than 1 million nonprofit tax returns. His aim was to look at how donors

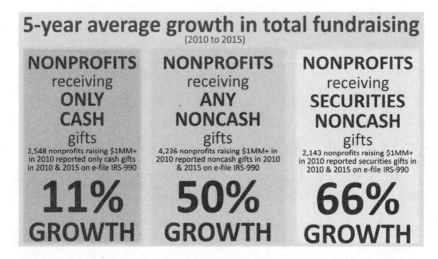

Figure 5.4   Growth in nonprofit organizations accepting stock donations

Source: Russell James III / pgcalc.com / CC BY-4.0.

were funding their charitable gifts. James found that nonprofit organizations that consistently received stock gifts grew six times faster than those receiving only cash.

Stock Donations Are Significantly Larger Than Cash Donations

When nonprofits ask for cash, they are most likely asking for gifts from the donor's "operating budget" that pay for routine monthly expenses. Inherently, the reference point for cash gifts from a donor's operating budget makes a psychological difference in evaluating the size of a gift. The same gift may seem material when compared to other operating budget purchases, but less significant when compared with the total wealth when including noncash assets. At Overflow, we have seen the generosity of donors of the clients we work with by seeing our average stock donation size currently being more than $10,000 compared to the US average $128 online donation.

Donors who have never made a gift from noncash assets may simply never have considered giving from wealth-holding assets rather than giving from spare operating income. Findings from experimental research show that people are much more willing to make charitable donations from irregular, unearned rewards (such as might occur with an appreciated asset) than from operating income (Russell, n.d.). It's therefore more important than ever to educate those donors on the benefits of noncash assets enabling nonprofits to open a new channel for donations.

Given the growth in stock donations, the number of noncash donations is accelerating quickly with more than 50% of all charitable donations coming from noncash assets between 2017 to 2020 (Fidelity Charitable, 2016). Nonprofits that intentionally pursue noncash gifts can generate both immediate tax benefits for donors and long-term fundraising growth benefits for the organization.

Launching and Scaling with Stock Donations

The time to reimagine fundraising is today! There are three major focus areas for nonprofits when launching and scaling stock donations:

- Internal processes for receiving and processing stock donations
- A simple and modern donation channel
- Donor education and awareness

As nonprofits consider stock donations as a prominent fundraising channel, they'll need to establish a brokerage account and a formal investment policy. Developing a comprehensive investment policy that outlines the full process for receiving, processing, and managing received stock donations is key in creating organizational alignment. The rest of this chapter explains how this can be done.

Creating an Internal Process to Receive Stock Donations

The way nonprofits have historically received stock donations (if they accepted stock donations at all) looks something like this:

1. Donor, an early Google employee, excitedly contacts the nonprofit to donate Facebook stock. Unfortunately, most nonprofits respond with "no," but for illustrative purposes, let's assume this nonprofit accepts stock.

2. The nonprofit tells the donor to navigate to the donor's brokerage website or call customer support to ask for a charitable stock transfer form. Unfortunately, the forms and requirements are unique to each brokerage and donation amount. The donor scrambles for a pen and paper to jot down the nonprofit's brokerage account number while on the phone.

3. Through a self-guided brokerage website tour, the donor finds the form and attempts to complete it.

4. The donor *prints* and signs the completed form and either puts it in an envelope to send via *snail mail* or *faxes* it to the brokerage.

5. The donor's brokerage receives the stock transfer form (finally) and reviews the information. Due to the stringent and constantly changing requirements, the forms are consistently filled out incorrectly, resulting in delays. The brokerage has to call the donor to resolve issues and often requires the donor to send a newly completed form to correct the errors.

6. Eventually, the donor brokerage initiates the transfer and the nonprofit receives the stock gift in its brokerage account from an "anonymous" donor.

7. The nonprofit then must decide whether to hold or liquidate the stock gift. It is critical to establish an investment policy and have a plan for receiving noncash assets.

8. The final step should be the nonprofit simply sends the generous donor a gift acknowledgment letter. However, it's not that simple with stock gifts. If the nonprofit receives an unprompted stock gift or has received multiple stock gifts, it has no clue which donor the gift belongs to. This results in a lost opportunity to engage with a high-value donor and creates additional time for the nonprofit team to generate a donor acknowledgment letter for the gift.

Phew. . . that was tiring.

The traditional method of accepting stock donations can be a slow, inaccurate, and painful process.

To receive a single stock gift, the nonprofit had to work with the donor individually to find the stock donation form, complete it, ensure the paperwork was correctly completed, track and record the gift, and send the donor acknowledgment letter. The complete lack of uniformity across brokerages in processing stock gifts manually prevents nonprofits from scaling this critical fundraising channel.

There is rarely a self-serve option for a donor to give stock. This creates additional pressure on the donor to sort out issues with their donation by having to call the broker and troubleshoot themselves. This can take months and can often be unsuccessful.

The worst part of this entire process is turning the positive experience of giving into a negative one for the donor. Donors want to be able to give quickly and efficiently while enjoying all the positive feelings and emotions that should come with being generous. A long and drawn-out manual process does not provide the elevated experience a donor wants and needs. According to research from Adrian Sageant, donors cite poor service or communication as the primary reason they stop giving to a nonprofit they have previously supported in the past (Planned Giving, n.d.).

With all the recent advances in technology, why are we still requiring a donor to print out and fax a form?

Why are we preventing donors from giving without needing to pick up the phone to call someone to initiate a gift?

A Simple and Modern Donation Channel

Nonprofit organizations seeking to receive stock donations should focus on providing a modern donor flow that supports frictionless giving to capture the donor's giving momentum.

The lightning-speed evolution of technology has transformed every aspect of our daily lives. Research now suggests that over 39% of donors contribute through an online giving platform (Fidelity Charitable, 2021). Just as the nonprofit space experienced a digital transformation in the way it accepted cash and credit donations, it's time we revolutionize the way we donate noncash assets. Donating stock has been stuck in the 20th century and it's more important than ever to bring it into the 21st century to meet the technological habits and needs of the next generation of donors. As such, enhancing the donor experience is critical to target a new segment.

Enhancing the donation flow caters to a critical new donor segment—millennials. Because millennials are tech-savvy, civic-oriented, and conscious of major societal trends across environmental, social, and economic issues, millennial donors are the fastest adopters of technology that makes everyday tasks in their daily lives instantaneous (Vogels, 2019). Providing a digital stock donation solution alongside existing cash donation flows enables millennials to think about stock giving in a whole new way.

A modern donation flow should be able to support the following:

1. Donors securely connect their brokerage account in seconds.
2. Donors' stock holdings are shown in a clear way to empower them to quickly select the stock they want to give.

3. The nonprofits' information is automatically captured and included in the giving flow.

4. Donor selects the shares, hits donate, digitally signs, and the gift is initiated with no further action.

5. The nonprofit receives the gift clearly tied to the donor, the critical donation information is automatically captured, a donor acknowledgment letter is generated, and the nonprofit simply has to review and send.

Providing a digital stock giving solution creates less friction for donors to give and increases the likelihood that donors will routinely give via stock. The automation enables nonprofits to save critical staff and volunteer time in processing and reporting received stock donations. This frees up time to focus on other initiatives that drive the nonprofit's mission forward.

Implementing modern stock donation technology is just the first step. And as I mentioned in Chapter 4, the best way to do this is to simply partner with a technology platform like Overflow that has already built the front-end and back-office tooling to enable this for your organization. Platforms like Overflow have teams that can collaborate with your IT or website admin to easily install the giving solution on your website as well as train key staff on how to manage the giving on the back end. On the front end, placement and consistency across all donation channels are critical for success in stock donations.

Placement of Stock Giving Options

One of the key factors in succeeding with stock fundraising is to ensure the stock giving option is placed alongside cash and credit giving buttons on the website. Donors, especially millennials and Gen Zers, are accustomed to minimal clicks to give cash, and the more time a potential donor has to spend digging through an "other ways to give" page, the less likely they are to donate.

Nonprofits eager to receive stock donations should place the "Donate Stock" button right next to the cash giving options.

There are three key focus areas for successful placement and donation flow:

- **Prominence**
  - The two or fewer touchpoints and clicks to arrive at the "Give Stock Button" is ideal.
- **Clear language**
  - Clear labeling to set expectations for the donor when the button is clicked. Clearly labeling the asset class for the button such as "Give Stock" is ideal.
- **Education and awareness in the giving flow**
  - Giving via stock or crypto is a new concept for many donors. Add a message such as "Maximize the impact of your donation and increase your tax savings by donating stock (crypto) directly."

With the right placement, nonprofits can drastically increase stock giving conversion rates, triggering a new funding stream from the existing donor base. Providing education and awareness as part of the actual donation flow is important, but it is critical that stock-giving awareness occurs before a donor even enters the donation flow.

Donor Awareness and Education

The primary barrier for a high-value donor gifting stock is the lack of awareness that nonprofits have the technology and processes in place to accept stock. *In addition, most donors are not aware that stock giving is the most tax-efficient way to give.* The combination of (1) giving from different assets stored outside of a checking account used for everyday expenses and (2) the significant tax benefits stock giving provides creates a win–win proposition for donors.

Nonprofits should provide donors with content focused on stock donations in communications, on their website, and at major fund-raising events. In a recent study conducted by Overflow, donors were asked what copy would entice them to donate stock. The survey choices included the following:

A. Increase your gift by up to **20%** by giving stock instead of selling to donate cash
B. Maximize your gift with stock
C. Increase your impact with zero additional cost to you
D. Save more on taxes by gifting stock
E. Donate stock

The results are shown in Figure 5.5.

Increasing a donor's gift up to 20% by giving stock instead of cash was the clear winner. Using sample language like the following will be effective in creating a hook for the donor when evaluating a potential stock donation.

Which bit of copy will get you most likely to click on the stock banner?

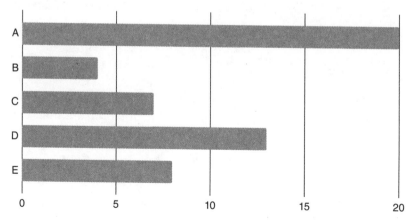

Figure 5.5   Survey results on best copy for stock giving engagement

Do not sell stock in order to donate cash. Donating appreciated stock held for more than a year allows you to give more by potentially saving up to 20% on capital gain taxes.

There is a small percentage of donors who truly understand the tax benefits in a way that drives consistent stock donations. Therefore, it is crucial for nonprofits to provide high-level education on the potential tax benefits and highlight that stock is the most tax-efficient way to give. However, it is also important to encourage donors to be intentional in evaluating the overall tax impact of their charitable giving plan with a CPA, wealth manager, or TurboTax analysis. (*Overflow is not a tax advisor. Please consult a tax professional for information about any potential tax implications associated with charitable giving.*)

Stock giving tax education spans three major cornerstones: (1) tax efficiency, (2) ease of giving, and (3) maximizing impact.

Tax Efficiency

- Eager to make an outsized impact today? Donating stock is the most tax-efficient way to give.
- Excited that your stock portfolio has appreciated over the past few years? Make a larger impact by donating your appreciated stock directly to our organization through significant tax savings.

Ease of Giving

- Donating appreciated stock assets allows you to maximize your impact while saving more on taxes. Our organization makes it easy. Donate today.
- "Share a Share" through frictionless stock giving. Our organization supports frictionless stock giving to support the causes you care about.

Maximizing Impact

- Deepen your impact and increase your tax savings when donating stock directly to [Nonprofit].
- Don't want to wait until [event date] to support [Nonprofit]? Deepen your impact and increase your tax savings today when donating stock.

Consistency Across Platforms Elevates Awareness

Nonprofits can raise awareness for stock donations through an omnichannel (or multichannel) messaging approach. Nonprofits should engage with donors through marketing campaigns across social media accounts, email communications, newsletters, and content pieces. Consistent communication provides donors with a constant reminder that stock donations should be top of mind.

Following are some helpful tips in building awareness across these channels:

Email

- Any time a nonprofit includes an ask in an email or has a link to donate, make sure that link leads directly to a giving page that includes a stock donation option.
- Include taglines such as "Maximize your impact with stock donations."
- Increase communications when the stock market has recently increased.

Social Media

- Build stock giving into the social media calendar to advertise stock giving.

- When making a fundraising request to followers, explicitly include stock giving as an option.
- Highlight tax savings donors have realized by donating stock.
- Include a direct giving link in the social media bio or "About Us" section.

Events

- Include a way for donors to buy tickets using stock donations.
- Highlight stock giving as an option on the "Call to Action" giving slide.
- Add a QR code on posters and flyers with a direct link to stock donations.

Content Pieces

- Add QR code that links to your stock giving page on each of these physical content pieces:
  - Brochures
  - Fliers
  - Schedules
  - Announcements

Now that we've taken a deep dive into stock and crypto giving and you've learned how to unlock net new generosity through these chapters, in Chapter 6 we will provide you seven master-level tactics to maximize giving overall.

6

Seven Master-Level Tactics to Maximize Giving

Thus far, we've discussed unlocking unprecedented levels of generosity at a high level. We've walked through how important it is to understand how the next generation thinks about giving. We've discussed alternative assets with a deep dive in cryptocurrency and stock donations, giving detailed playbooks and insights about how to execute that well.

Now, it's time to go to the next level. In this chapter, I will give you seven master-level tactics that I believe can really change the game in terms of maximizing giving overall.

Here are the seven tactics:

- **Save on credit, debit and ACH merchant processing fees.**
  - This will cover anything connected to online giving as it relates to a checking, savings account, or credit card. There are a lot of opportunities to save on credit fees, and I will give you a deep dive on the background on this and how to think about it.
- **Teach the tithe.**
  - Though the tithe is a church-specific principle, we can take some core principles of it from the nonprofit space as well.
- **Identify high-capacity potential givers who are not yet giving.**
  - A lot of times you'll experience the 80/20 rule, where 20% of your supporters are doing 80% of meeting the budget and doing the heavy lifting in terms of giving, but you have so many more potential givers. Perform an analysis on who might be added to your pool of donors.
- **Take advantage of corporate matching benefits.**
  - This is a low-effort, high-impact opportunity. I will break down the concrete stats about how much corporate matching goes unmatched in the United States.

- **Explain IRA required minimum distributions.**
  - People who have retired are actually required to take certain levels of distributions that go underused because they don't want to get taxed on them. This can be another source of donations.
- **Take advantage of wills, trusts, and legacy giving.**
  - This can be really important for your organization. I will give you the IRS stats on how much money is given through bequests.
- **Create a line of sponsorship revenue at events.**
  - I will tell you how you can create a line of revenue by taking advantage of sponsorships at conferences and events that your organization puts on.

Save on credit, debit and ACH merchant processing fees.

This first point contains vital information to make sure that your organization does not lose key donor revenue to the various fees charged by financial institutions. First, let's understand the presence of fees is not the problem. Let me explain.

Why Are "Cash Processing Fees" Collected in the First Place?

For most transactions in our society, there's a third party (or merchant services provider) that handles the nitty gritty of said transaction. That includes communicating with the banks/financial institutions, safeguarding against security breaches, and ensuring the transaction is legit.

In exchange for their services (which often provide accessibility and convenience), these third parties often collect a transaction or processing fee.

As a church or nonprofit organization, you want every dollar to be going toward your mission or purpose, and you don't want donors to be dissuaded by "arbitrary" fees or nickel-and-diming.

"Whenever we've talked to a lot of churches, they'll say, 'I don't want to pay the 3–5% processing fee.' They want to push people to give via check," said Derek Neece, vice president of business development at Overflow and board member at the Association of Related Churches (ARC).

Processing fees are often a sticking point for both the organization/charity and potential donor. However, understanding how the system works and why certain fees are necessary is essential before you can unlock rates that both help you meet your needs and keep donors happy.

Electronic Processing Versus Cash/Check Processing

It's a common church experience to have a bucket or plate passed around for the offering and end up with a bunch of cash or checks. A similar experience to this can happen at a charity event or gala where checks are written and submitted within the night. Both the giver and the organization may think this cuts out the "middleperson" as the exchange is happening straight from the giver to the receiver.

However, that doesn't mean there isn't an additional cost attached to it. As Neece explains:

> What [people] don't realize is there's a cost to that check and that the processing fee that that check goes through as well. Meaning if a church passes buckets and 90% of people give a check, there is a count that has to happen where people are counting those funds and those checks. There's a person that's being paid hourly to enter that data manually into the giving solution. They have to run that check to the bank, and there's even a security risk to that deposit being in hand, rather than just automatically depositing it to the bank.

Basically, there's arguably more work that goes into accounting for these donations manually, as it's someone's job to account for cash and check donations.

On the flip side, many churches and nonprofits have moved toward accepting gifts electronically. It's widely known that this is a more convenient and secure way to give, but some don't understand why there are various fees attached, nor where those extra fees actually go.

Let's break it down.

These platforms often have a processing fee that typically ranges from 2–9%. But the first thing to clear up is that these organizations aren't just taking that extra money and pocketing it. Many organizations accept credit, debit, or "electronic funds transfers." Card providers such as Visa charge the organization a fee and in turn the organization pays a fee to securely store your card data with the payment gateway.

These are called interchange fees, or in other words, fees that the organization, charity, or church pays to accept credit card donations in the first place. Per Merchant Maverick, "interchange fees cover the risk of fraud for a transaction, plus handling costs for sending the payment to the acquiring bank and, ultimately, the merchant's bank account" (Kehl, 2022).

So although it may seem like these fees are arbitrary, they're actually covering a lot of different bases, from security to proper accounting of your money.

Fees aside, there's a time cost to give via check or cash. If you give through a credit card through Overflow, for instance, it's a next business day deposit. With a check, someone typically has to go deposit it. It can take anywhere from five to seven business days to fully settle, depending on the processor and the bank.

Beyond that, electronic recurring giving reduces the likelihood of "churn," or a potential holdup or hesitation to give. Instead of having to choose every Sunday or every month whether or not they want to be generous, the donor sets up everything at the beginning of the year and it almost becomes out of sight, out of mind.

People may be less worried about processing fees when they've planned out their giving in advance and fully accounted for what their giving entails, versus getting sticker shock or cold feet in a single act of giving. Our moods, feelings, and situations can change rapidly, and the fervency to give can quickly dissolve if it's either challenging or inconvenient to give in the first place. So while the existence of fees is not the problem, ensuring you find a platform and solution that can give you the best fees is key.

Finding the Best Processing Fee Rates

If you look across different giving platforms, you'll notice some variety in processing fees. For example:

- Indiegogo, a crowd-funding resource, charges a 6.75% platform and processing fee that gets marked down to 3% if the campaign's goal is met.
- Pushpay, a donor management system for the church space, charges up to 3.5–3.8% on its card processing fees.
- JustGiving, a social platform for giving, charges a 5% platform fee plus a 2.9% processing fee.

Part of the reason there are higher fees across different giving competitors is that 90% are tied to Stripe, which has a fixed fee that they must get above to make money. Stripe charges 2.9% + 30 cents for card transactions, and 2.7% plus 2.7% + 5 cents for in-person payments.

Something that we have been passionate about at Overflow is to find a way to minimize these fees to be as low as possible. Typically, we can beat any processing rate because we're more closely tied to what Visa, American Express, MasterCard, and so on charge: 1.29% + $0.05 to 2.54% + 10 cents on average per transaction. It's the direct relationships we have been able to cultivate in the last several years with certain payment processors that have enabled us to do this for our customers.

When our customers start searching and switching to platforms like ours to save on merchant fees, they typically see about 1% in fee savings across the year blended across transactions. If you are processing $10,000,000 in online giving a year, that is $100,000 in savings! In the nonprofit world that equates to a top talent hire.

Other factors you should be thinking about with your online giving cash processing:

- **Taking out the middle person.** Stripe is popular because it offers the giving infrastructure and payment processing software that most organizations or businesses lack. However, it charges fees based off of the interchange that it's tied to. Because we already have a giving infrastructure built, we are positioned to take out the middle person.
- **Accepting automatic clearing house (ACH) payments.** A focus on accepting ACH transfers, which is basically just money sent directly from bank to bank through the ACH network. Most ACH transfers come without any kind of additional fee, or at least very minimal fees.
- **Simplicity.** It's been said that if it takes more than three steps, the purchase or gift likely won't be made. If there are too many barriers to entry, people won't follow through.

Ultimately, while we've been primarily talking about unlocking net new giving in the book, a master-level tactic to maximize giving is to also analyze your bottom line and optimize for net new savings where it's possible. Oftentimes, one of the biggest needle movers is switching your payment processing to a platform that can save you significantly in that area.

Teach the Tithe

Specifically for churches, the biggest way to move the needle in your giving is to focus on the tithe.

Something that we do every year at VIVE Church is that we dedicate the month of October to teaching biblically about the tithe.

A lot of myths surround the tithe, such as the idea that the tithe is a tax to be able to go to church, or that it's just a way to get money from the people of the church. Others say that the tithe is law, while we're meant to be based on grace, or that the tithe is Old Testament while we're meant to be based in the New Testament. Ultimately, these are all excuses and diversions from what the principle of the tithe actually represents.

The principle of the tithe is not a tax; it's not even a requirement of Christian living. In the New Testament we are based on the premise of grace, not law. In saying that, the introduction of the tithe, biblically, was prelaw, before the ten commandments, even before Moses. The introduction of the tithe came from Abraham.

Abraham was a man who had gone into battle and won a victory. Because he won the victory, he acknowledged that the source of his victory was God. The bible says that Abraham then gave a tithe of the spoils he had won in that battle back to the high priest, who at the time was a representation of your relationship with God. It was, simply, a recognition that, "I wouldn't have gotten the victory without God. It is *because* of God that I have victory."

This is an important truth to understand. At the end of the day, somebody will tithe consistently, on a recurring basis, sustainably, as a part of their lifestyle and the fabric of their identity once they have the revelation that everything is not their own. That all of their provision, all of their income, the reason they're living, is because of God. With that understanding, people can see that the tithe is not even giving; it's returning back a portion of what God has given them. The tithe, specifically, is taught to go to the storehouse, the place where you get spiritually fed. Today, that is the local church. The New Testament says, "Where your treasure is, is where your heart is also" (Matthew 6:21). What a very interesting understanding of what money does to us on a psychological level.

In the research for the science of generosity, which I previously discussed in Chapter 2, it was found that when you give financially, it releases a dopamine in your brain on the level of when you get to shelter or when you eat food. So even our bodies, our physiological makeup, are aligned to the fact that wherever you align your finances, you also align your heart and your spirit.

This is the base spiritual component. On a more pragmatic level, this is what moves the needle the most. You can do so many galas, put on the fanciest events, but if you don't have a core set of people and if you're not growing that set of people to understand the tithe, then you are actually not doing the most impactful thing for your organization.

There is a Silicon Valley term for this. Now, not to make this crass, because the church and nonprofit organizations are not businesses, but they *are* corporate entities. And how we refer to this in Silicon Valley terms is *annual recurring revenue*, or *subscriptions*.

Think about Netflix. Netflix could try to get you to pay a la carte for every movie, but what's better is predictability. What's better is them putting their whole catalog out there so you can access anything in the catalog for a set subscription rate. Locking in subscribers gives them predictability to be able to plan their business accordingly. In the same way, churches and nonprofits need to think about not just trying to maximize one-time gifts, but focusing on recurring giving, really focusing on the deeper principle of why someone would give on a recurring basis.

Nonprofits can learn from the tithe. If the church has been able to grow a membership that has the conviction to give 10% of their income every single month, year over year, nonprofits can understand what's possible.

Three Lessons Nonprofits Can Learn from the Tithe

- **Conviction is possible.** It's possible for a set of people to be so convicted and have such a revelation about giving that they will give up to 10% or even more toward a cause that they care about because they want to live a purpose-driven life.

- **The best giving is out of gratitude.** The tithe highlights a key understanding that those who are giving in the church: give from a place of gratitude. Cultivating a culture of gratitude within your giving community is vital. When most people give to nonprofits, they're giving based on guilt or in response to catastrophe. That's not always bad and can definitely be leveraged, but what's more powerful than guilt giving is gratitude-based giving. Not, "I'm giving because it's my responsibility; I have so much that I have to give some," because when someone is guilt-giving they're giving out of their leftovers. When someone is giving out of gratitude, it's "I understand that I am blesssed beyond measure so out of that gratitude I will give out of an overflow."

- **Focus on the core.** A lot of times, nonprofits can get so caught up in focusing on maximizing their reach that they can forget to focus on the core. But many times the biggest needle mover in your organization can be focusing on those who are currently giving just a tip, not a tithe. When you give them a deeper revelation about the organization, you can take them on a journey from being a <1% of their income giver to up to a 10% of their income giver.

Identify High-Capacity Potential Givers Who Are Not Yet Giving

If your goal is to grow your fundraising ability within your organization, are you examining the givers you already have to understand their current giving versus their giving capacity? Many organizations leave a lot on the table because they focus more on attracting new donors or volunteers than on growing and maximizing the ones they already have.

To even have a view of how well you know your community, you have to get your tools right and choose a customer relationship management platform (CRM) that can help you manage the activity of your donors.

Examples of CRM Platforms

- Salesforce
- Virtuous
- Planning Center Online (for churches)
- Bloomerang (for nonprofits)

You want to understand where there is high activity. Maybe you have people who are volunteering, maybe people who are giving on some level.

Next, you want to take that data and overlay it on some sort of wealth management tool. Overflow offers wealth management tool services in which we can analyze the potential net worth of a volunteer or an individual who has given something based on factors we can pull in from third-party resources and run through our algorithm. This can potentially be correlated to their capacity to give.

Not enough organizations focus on segments within their current supporting base, whether they're volunteers or people who have given before, and try to cultivate relationships and personalize value for those individuals to activate them at a higher level. This is key. One thing I see is that so many organizations go the spray-and-pray route, where they give one broadcast-level message to their whole community. With the right data, you can customize and personalize communications to specific segments in hopes to deepen relationship, deepen value, and speak to specific things that can give them deeper purpose to unlock bigger giving.

A lot of times your goal may be to grow your followership and your donor base, but sometimes the gold is already in your current list. You just haven't dug deep enough to be able to find the gold within your current supporter base. You haven't given them enough attention or personalization.

Here's the thing. You can add another 10,000 donors to your donor base and barely move the needle. Those new donors might give a few dollars one-time and never again.

You have to understand your systems and processes to be able to honor and steward the people who have already come to you. Focus on activating them at a deeper level before you ask for more. I like to use the analogy of a bucket. There's no sense in continuing to pour water in the bucket if you have too many holes, too many cracks, and too many leaks. It's going to stay a leaky bucket. For Silicon Valley B2B Software-as-a-Service startups, we are actually evaluated on our ability to retain and expand users or customers. 100% retention is actually not enough. What's considered "good" is 120%. Why? Because a truly satisfied user or customer is not only retained but expand their relationship with the company by their willingness to pay more for additional features and services year over year. Instead of focusing too heavily on new donors if you have a "leaky bucket" you should disproportionately focus on solving the leaky bucket first so that you know that when new donors come they will stick and deepen their commitment over time.

Take Advantage of Corporate Matching Benefits

Let's talk about free money that organizations are not getting right now (see Figure 6.1).

Each year $4 to $7 billion goes unmatched! This means not enough people are taking advantage of their corporate match benefit and the "free money" is gone because it is a use-it-or-lose-it model annually.

There are so many Fortune 500 companies and beyond that have what's called corporate gift matching benefit. Companies like Google, Facebook, and Apple will match up to $10,000 of donations based on what their employees donate. My company Overflow also has a corporate gift matching benefit! Many of these corporate organizations use a platform to manage their corporate giving, such as Benevity, to facilitate these matches.

For you to receive this money, your donors need to be able to partner with their HR team, understand the process, and know how

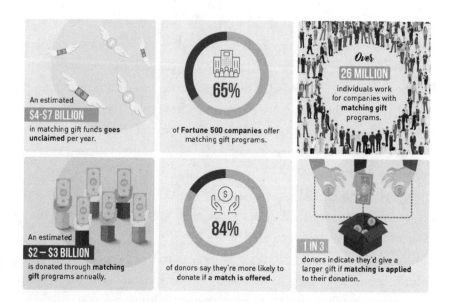

Figure 6.1   Double the Donation identifies estimation of unmatched giving every year

Source: Double the Donation (n.d.).

to apply for it so that every dollar they give to your organization to a certain threshold is doubled.

You can take advantage of this corporate benefit—for a nonprofit organization, it's about educating your donors that they have this at their disposal, especially if they work for a Fortune 500, tech, or consumer product goods company. They're already giving to you; why not do two minutes of work to email HR, or fill out the form, or submit the paperwork to be able to gain approval and distribution of a corporate match? Somebody's $10,000 gift in one year could become $20,000 if they just did that work, but they won't know to do that work if they haven't heard from you about it.

This isn't a top-of-mind process for your donors. They may never have heard of it and might not know to look up if their company offers this. People are busy. You want to make this super easy for them. Going one step further, platforms like Overflow can help nonprofits automate this education and automate the process at time of transaction. That's another option to explore.

This could mean six to seven figures of additional free money if your organization develops a process.

The Process

Look at your current donations, transactions, and donors. Remember, a CRM platform, which we just discussed, is key to be able to easily analyze this and pull reports of this activity. You can use tools like Overflow that will overlay the type of companies that these donors work at, and you can give two levels of communication.

- **General communication.** Let your whole donor base know to look up their company's corporate match policy to double their donation today and maximize their impact before year's end. I would do this about September, October, or November. You can also tie and remind them what $1, $100, $1,000 will do in terms of impact to compel them to do the two minutes of work to find out about their corporate gift match. You can even be specific, with messaging such as, "Two minutes of work could potentially build three wells when your company matching program matches your gift."

- **Use CRM data.** This is next level. Use your company's CRM to send out personalized messaging. For example, "Hey, Mr. Vance Roush, thank you for your $5,000 gift this year. We saw that you work at Google, and we know that Google's corporate gift matching policy matches up to $10,000. If you simply apply for a corporate gift match through your HR team at Google, they will instantly gift match your gift before the end of the year, doubling your donation to $10,000. With that $10,000 we will be able to. . . ." This level of personalization requires the CRM and financial platform overlay I discussed in the previous section, but it has the opportunity to spur immediate action.

However you do it, stop leaving money on the table and create a plan for how your organization will take advantage of corporate gift matching benefits moving forward.

Explain IRA Required Minimum Distributions

Let's discuss required minimum distributions (RMD for short). Many probably know the term IRA, an investment retirement account. I won't go too deep into it here, but there are multiple types of retirement accounts. One specific thing I want to highlight is the power of understanding, on a high level, how IRAs operate when someone retires and how to really connect and direct your older donors to have an impact and live a life of purpose and legacy toward the latter part of their journey.

What is so fascinating is that for decades, people contributed to their IRA as a way of minimizing taxes. So, there is this mentality of trying to minimize taxes as much as possible and defer them toward retirement. Now, some people get to their twilight years and find they've actually done quite well, so they don't necessarily need the full distributions of their IRA every year. But there is this provision called required minimum distribution (RMD), in which depending on the regulation, the IRA holder still needs to withdraw a certain amount. If they don't, they actually lose that money.

The reason some people won't take a certain amount of distribution is that if they don't need it, they don't want to get taxed on it. After all, as I said, they have a tax minimization mentality. What they could do, though, instead of withdrawing it and facing the taxes or losing it, is to take the portion they don't need to use and directly donate it.

This is a win–win situation.

If they directly donate a portion of that RMD to a charity or nonprofit—hopefully your organization if you're the ones to educate them about this—they can take a charitable tax deduction, which enables them to further minimize their taxes while also making an impact in using it for good.

This is another master-class tactic to maximize giving.

Take Advantage of Wills, Trusts, and Legacy Giving

Bequests are a distribution from the portion of someone's estate that has been dedicated to charity or charitable purposes for a specific organization. Literally billions of dollars every year is given through bequests towards organizations when people pass away.

The opportunity for your organization is massive. There is still 43.9% of nonprofits that don't focus any fundraising/gift nurturing on gifts in wills or estate gifts. And yet . . . more than 85% of all planned gifts are made via a will or a trust, meaning charitable bequests (per Bloomerang, a top nonprofit CRM provider).

Per Charity Navigator, annual bequest giving represents over $35 billion! That is 5%–10% of total giving in any given year.

Now, millennials aren't thinking as much about the end of their lives. But what's interesting is that more and more we're seeing tools like Overflow that enable people to create a free will. Through the creation of a free will, someone can directly determine what percentage of their estate they want to donate at the end of their life and to which organization.

Hopefully your organization is signed up through a platform like Overflow, so that you can be highlighted at that point of decision.

Wills and trusts are powerful, and it's crucial for you to understand their power. At the end of the day, especially for those who have come into means and are on a trajectory to have an estate, they're in a mindset of not just the here and now but future generations and legacy. They don't necessarily need to, or even want to, pass on all of their wealth to one person or family, even if it's their children. They want their legacy to be beyond family and go toward a larger cause, something they really care about. Whether it's climate change, a faith-based community, a humanitarian effort—this is why people put their names on buildings at universities: they want their legacy to live on. They want their life's work to mean something beyond a nice lifestyle for themselves. They're asking how their contributions will serve and unlock others.

When you talk about legacy giving, nothing is as tied to legacy as your will and your trust. Understand that it can be simply a conversation to ensure your organization is positioned as a beneficiary of a donor's will or trust.

Accomplishing that goal takes incredible nuance, intelligence, and the right context. In a lot of ways, we try to scale this through technology at Overflow. We try to serve generations such as millennials, who maybe don't want to hire a lawyer to build a will, by offering them a service to make a free will. As they're making that will, gaining a value add from our service, at the very end we can simply prompt them to include a commitment for an organization they love.

If this free will service is a button on an organization's website and someone gets this free service through that organization's website, that organization will be top of mind for that person during their will-creation process. So when that prompt comes up, their mindset is "Thank you [Nonprofit Organization] for providing me this service so that I can easily create my will . . . sure I'd love to dedicate X% of my estate towards you as a legacy!"

That is a huge way to maximize giving.

Obviously, these are not finances that your organization will receive tomorrow, especially if a millennial is creating a will. You might not see these funds for 30 to 50 years. But think about your organization outlasting even your involvement in it. Your organization is important. Churches, charities, cause-based organizations—we hope these organizations live on and thrive for hundreds of years. Harvard and other universities thought about this decades ago. They created endowments and legacy gift programs and positioned themselves to be beneficiaries of estates, so now they're set up for hundreds of years. You have the opportunity to help your organization do the same.

Create a Line of Sponsorship Revenue at Events

This last master-level tactic to maximize giving is one that people don't really think about. Do you have a conference? Should your organization create a conference or some sort of event or gathering? Whether it's a conference focused on women, a conference for your organization, a conference focused on a specific set of people or industries within your supporter base, is there a subject matter expertise or something marketable within your supporter base that people would get value from?

If you're going to hold a conference, whether it's a large event with more than a thousand people or a smaller event with a niche, important group such as decision-makers or high-caliber people of a certain industry, you have an opportunity to drive additional cash flow through sponsorship. With research, your organization can curate a set of relationships with companies who want to sponsor your event to have a chance to reach your invitees.

Sponsorship revenue is sometimes underestimated. Sometimes the right sponsors can unlock incredible amounts of resources. Companies are hungry for opportunities to deploy capital that will yield them and ROI on marketing spend. If they can get in front of a set of potential buyers/customers/users, that is a golden opportunity for them.

This doesn't just mean product-based companies. Consider those, but also real estate companies or financial advisors who are always looking for clients. Companies have significant marketing budgets, and they're finding that deploying money on platforms such as social media or Google ads are starting to provide diminishing returns. They're not seeing ROI on online tactics that used to work. Instead, they are seeing ROI in places that are highly relational, where there's deep connections that can be made. The conversion rates are higher in the context of community.

What better way to have contextual-based marketing than at a conference that's tied to a church or a nonprofit or a cause-based organization that the community trusts? The key will be to curate these sponsors and to vet them to ensure their quality so you do not risk damaging the trust you have instilled in your community over years of serving them.

It's not uncommon for companies to have philanthropic budgets, and there's also a double bottom line here. Not only is sponsoring your event a marketing opportunity for them but there's also a feel-good factor—an opportunity to align their company with a deeper purpose that they really care about. That can also unlock larger sponsorships.

If you already have an event, this is a no-brainer. If you don't, seriously consider whether your organization should have an event or conference, with this being another line of resources, giving, and finances for your organization.

Now that you understand the power of alternative sources of and how to maximize giving covered in Chapters 3–6, you are ready to go beyond these strategies to the relationship aspect of fundraising. In Chapter 7, we will explore the donor experience and how the various ways your organization shows up for your community can affect and influence your ability to fundraise at the optimal levels.

7

The Donor Experience

Chapters 4–6 have emphasized cryptocurrency, stock donations, and cash processing, which are currently the three most important asset classes for nonprofit organizations to pursue in terms of value and in terms of what is donatable in the overall market. In order to leverage these assets to maximize fundraising in the Silicon Valley way, it is not enough to focus on understanding the various monetary inputs themselves. An organization must also know how to use these inputs to create an excellent donor experience.

What Is the Importance of the Donor Experience?

Nonprofit organizations have a responsibility to be as efficient as possible with the money that donors give to maximize the effect of that money toward achieving the organization's goal. This is the basis of a trustworthy organization and the defining characteristic of the donor experience. In order to earn and keep the donor's trust, and improve donor engagement and retention, the organization needs to focus on creating an experience that donors engage with continually and enthusiastically.

Many organizations believe that they have an excellent donor experience. However, the decisions made by leadership and staff reflect decision-making driven by what the organization wants. Think about customer service and how most customer service reps are incentivized to be loyal to their brand more than the customer and their needs. The most successful technology companies have truly taken a customer-first approach. Applying a Silicon Valley or e-commerce lens, the end donor or supporter of any nonprofit organization is ultimately that organization's customer.

At Overflow, we have built a platform that donors want because we understand that for a healthy amount of recurring and sustainable resources, an organization must understand what its customer—the donor—wants and how to make their experience better. Providing an intentionally crafted donor experience enables nonprofit organizations to maintain, grow, and accelerate their mission and vision.

Life travels at the speed of relationships, especially in the world of nonprofit. The challenge for a nonprofit organization that wants engaged donors and sustainable inflow is to look internally and assess how well it is actually cultivating the relationships with the donor.

Many organizations believe that they have a strong donor experience. They will cite the work they do to cultivate relationships or the care they show to their supporters. However, as a first measure of assessing how exceptional your donor experience truly is, I invite you to evaluate your website.

Ask yourself these questions:

- Is your website user friendly?
- Does your website provide the option to give using the asset classes discussed in Chapters 4–6?
- Does your website clearly display the mission of your organization in a compelling way?
- Is the website beautifully designed, in a way that draws supporters in?

All of these aspects demonstrate consideration of the donor experience at the level that it takes to truly earn and maintain donor trust and leverage that trust for sustainable inflow.

Figures 7.1, 7.2, and 7.3 show examples of a large nonprofit's website evaluated for its user experience through the lens of a Silicon Valley product manager—the person typically responsible for owning user web experience in the tech world. Use this as a reference for evaluating your own website.

This website's home page has great callouts for donating, which will lead you directly to online cash processing.

The footer is where you finally find other ways to give. Can you see it? You'll find it, but it's buried at the bottom.

Surprisingly, there is not one callout for stock donations, the largest noncash asset donation channel.

What is clear is that even if stock donations were called out, this website is not optimized for driving transactions through that channel. It is exclusively focused on driving online cash donations, which is what most nonprofits are optimized for, following the example of UNICEF, which is one of the largest NPOs in the world. This is an incredibly large missed opportunity.

Bloomerang, a top nonprofit CRM, summarized a breakthrough study that we referenced in Chapter 5 really well:

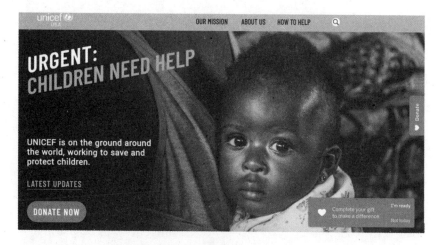

Figure 7.1   UNICEF give page

Source: UNICEF.

Figure 7.2   UNICEF footer

Source: UNICEF.

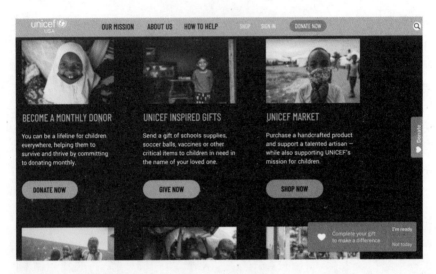

Figure 7.3   UNICEF ways to give

Source: UNICEF.

Dr. Russell James J.D., Ph.D., CFP®, professor in the Department of Personal Financial Planning at Texas Tech University, recently completed a landmark study reporting on data from 1 million NPO e-filed tax returns from more than 200,000 nonprofit organizations. What it revealed in terms of total growth in fundraising contributions over a five-year period (2010–2015) from different types of charities was nothing short of amazing.

- Received only cash gifts = achieved 11% growth. Just barely kept up with inflation.
- Received any kind of noncash gift = achieved 50% growth. Included gifts of personal and real property and deferred gifts.
- Received securities noncash gifts = achieved 66% growth. Massive difference from just this one strategy!

Organizations promoting and receiving stock gifts saw a positive 55% difference in growth from charities accepting just cash!

Based on the online user experience analyzed with UNICEF in the figures, I would say they are not aiming to optimize online stock donations which would be a missed opportunity based on Dr. James's study! Imagine if they optimized the experience to actually be able to receive these types of gifts online. According to James, the implications and impact would be massive.

What Are the Essential Principles to Craft an Excellent Donor Experience?

Though the website is vital, and a good tool to begin analyzing user experience, the donor experience is built on 10 key principles.

The following 10 principles must be deliberately managed for any organization to build deep relationships with their donors. These are 10 principles that every organization can execute against, that will lead to deeper relationships, and therefore will maximize the resources available to the organization:

- Vision
- Realistic, manageable time lines
- Tangible, clear impact
- Excellent execution
- Tapping into recurring giving
- Cadence of communication
- Story and testimony driven
- Clear, intentional brand
- Culture of generosity
- Intentional, aligned team

Vision

In the bible, a text I read often, there is a verse in Habakkuk that explains that without vision, the people perish. Whether you, personally, believe in the bible or not, this is true for your organization. If there is a lack of vision, or if the vision of your organization is not clear, your organization will start to deteriorate.

A strong vision is the hook that will hold together your organization internally and externally. This is what you are energizing donors with to part with their money for and motivating your employees to show up every day to work toward. A strong vision will propel your organization forward. A lack of vision, or poor vision, will have a negative impact internally that will then extend to a negative experience for your donors.

The following are signs that your vision isn't strong enough:

- A lack of responsibility or ownership within your team
- A lack of enthusiasm from volunteers
- Difficulty meeting fundraising goals

On the other side, when your vision is strong:

- Team takes ownership, choosing to go above and beyond.
- Volunteers are energized to do more than asked.
- Donors give passionately and consistently.

A strong vision is more than an exciting or heartwarming statement or memo. Additionally, the vision must be proportionally bigger than the fundraising goal. In Silicon Valley, investors are primarily interested in billion-dollar ideas. This means that for a $10 million fundraising ask, typically coined a Series A fundraising round, you cannot have a $10 million vision. You need a billion-dollar vision. To ask for $10 million dollars from your supporters, you must illustrate how your organization will have a billion dollars' worth of impact in the world.

Asking for money means asking people to give up money that they could be using to affect their own lives or to affect something else instead. This is especially impactful for many nonprofit donations where this money is given away, often to causes that will not tangibly benefit the giver. The organization must then deliver intangible benefit by motivating the donor with a vision that delivers over and above the financial ask. While you may not be able to deliver a return on investment, you can certainly still deliver ROI—return on impact—and you must capture this within the framework of how you share your vision!

Realistic, Manageable Time Lines

A billion-dollar vision and consistent, transparent execution are the way your organization earns the respect and trust of donors. However, it is very difficult for any community to rally around something when a project time line is ambiguous.

One principle that always holds true, whether within the faith community, philanthropic community, or corporate financial community, is that nothing gets done without a deadline. Internally, your vision needs to be time-bound and have a clear deadline for execution.

When communicating vision to your support community, it is not enough to have a deadline, but it must also be correctly structured to motivate donors. It is good to have a big vision. But let's say your organization has a 50-year vision. Whoever is communicating this vision must have the ability to break that long-term vision into smaller increments.

Your organization should have a new one-year vision every year, as well as an ongoing five-year and ten-year vision. If the vision of your organization is too long term, your organization's supporters cannot rally around it. Breaking your vision down into steps with shorter time lines enables your community to buy into your vision, and also enables you to build the consistency of execution necessary to foster credibility and demonstrate the character of your organization. Being able to break down a large, long-term vision into manageable steps is the difference between selling a dream and truly rallying a community to give in support of a vision that can be executed on.

Tangible, Clear Impact

How does your donor community understand the impact that their donations are having toward your vision?

In order for your execution to matter to your donors, your organization has to have impact. If the people who give to your organization cannot see the relationship between their dollars and the change your organization is creating, you have not effectively communicated impact.

Notice in Figure 7.4 the call out: "Your $40.00 monthly donation can give 12 people clean water every year."

Charity: Water is a brilliant example of tying a specific amount to an impressive level of impact that will help drive a decision to give. For a lot of people, $40 is in the realm of possibility, and that amount is especially compelling if it translates to 12 human beings receiving clean water!

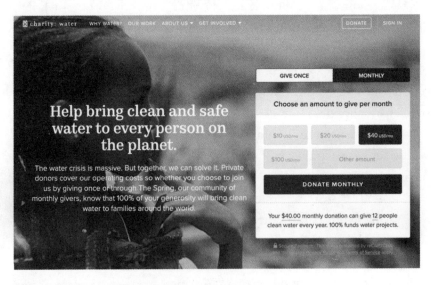

Figure 7.4   Charity: Water donation page

Source: Charity Global, Inc.

As Figure 7.5 shows, at Overflow we've worked with organizations to take this principle next level and tie it to what a simple stock donation could do.

At the time of this social media post, a share of Google could be given and liquidated and the cash value could buy internet-enabled laptops for two students to learn coding through Streetcode.

At the time of the social media post shown in Figure 7.6, a share of Tesla could be given and liquidated, and the cash value could save a heart through American Heart Association.

These organizations operate in different spheres and are working toward different goals, yet all have created a clear equation where supporters see the direct tie between the exact amount of money they give and the exact amount of impact they have. Work to understand the direct impact that donor dollars have on your mission and vision, and find an effective way to communicate that.

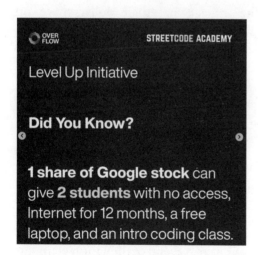

Figure 7.5   Overflow example Instagram post about Streetcode

Source: Overflow Instagram Profile.

Figure 7.6   Overflow example Instagram post about the American Heart Association

Source: Overflow Instagram Profile.

When donors can see the impact that their dollars have on achieving the vision, they are motivated to give, and to give at higher levels.

Excellent Execution

In my experience as the chief financial officer of VIVE Church, the reason we are able to raise more money each and every year is because we always do what we say we are going to do. When we deliver our vision to the church, we then execute that vision fully and transparently relay the results back to our organization within the next 12 months.

This is not always easy. Following are several of the vision elements we have had as a church that we have communicated about and executed on.

- In 2013 we introduced our five-by-five vision: to plant a new church location every year for five years. We achieved this by launching Palo Alto, San Jose, San Francisco, Oakland, and Rome, Italy.

- In 2018 we introduced our five-by-one vision, to plant five new church locations in one year. That was the year we ended up planting churches in Chicago, Austin, Honolulu, Morgan Hill (now South Valley), and Milan, Italy. All 10 locations are still going, and we've never shut down a campus.

- In 2019 our vision was to raise $200,000 to eradicate $20 million worth of medical debt. We partnered with RIP Medical Debt (a 501c3 organization), and in that partnership we ended up forgiving $19 million worth of medical debt in the Chicago area alone, resulting in *Relevant Magazine* writing an article about our church.

- Throughout the years we've had a multistage initiative to bring a high-quality online stream. Over several years we've raised funds for broadcast equipment and technology, as well the capacity to be able to hire pastors to be able to focus on online ministry full time. To date we have hundreds of thousands of views and real people being impacted by our online ministry, for example, a member of our church in Turkey who can only receive the gospel through the internet and has found specific discipleship through our online services.

- In 2021 our vision was to purchase a $32 million building in Mountain View, California, across the street from Google, which required raising several million dollars in 45 days. Because of the trust from our community people sacrificed immensely, from children starting businesses to families selling their homes, and we were able to honor their sacrifice by fulfilling on the promise and purchasing the building.

I share this to highlight our consistency, because that consistency is what has propelled us forward. Our ability to increase the capacity of our fundraising is directly correlated to our credibility and character as an organization. Because we do what we say we are going to do in one year, our donors believe that when they give again as we update our vision, we will once again deliver on the promise.

Being consistent and transparent in your execution will foster trust between your organization and your supporters. Again, if you adopt a Silicon Valley mindset and view your supporters as your customers, delivering on what you promise your customer is the only way to ensure your customer returns. Not only that, but as that credibility grows, donors voluntarily give more to the vision, because they know that their donations are well managed and therefore their money is well used.

Vision is key, but continued trust is not fostered solely based on what you say you will do but is also dependent on *doing* what you say you will do.

Tapping into Recurring Giving

Most organizations are primarily focused on event-based fundraising. There are several benefits of event-based fundraising. It can be very catalytic, because having donors in the room can create a sense of momentum and urgency that leads to higher donations. It can also provide a very concentrated giving event, with organizations able to pull large amounts of donations in one night toward a vision. However, it can also become stressful and ineffective, especially if the organization relies too much on event-based giving, because these are typically one-time donor gifts.

When your organization is reliant on one-time, in-person giving events, what happens when you have an event such as the recent global pandemic? Though this was a more extreme example, it highlights how unstable and insecure event-based giving is as the linchpin of an organization's donation strategy.

Something that all nonprofit organizations can learn from the church space is the concept of recurring giving.

Historically, the church has done well fostering recurring giving. Annual charitable contributions to 501(c)3 organizations total roughly $450 billion a year. Of this, 30% is given to the local church, roughly $135 billion a year. After the church, the next highest contribution is 13% to educational causes, which totals $58.5 billion, a difference of $76.5 billion dollars. The church, fueled by recurring giving, understands something fundamental about the human experience.

As discussed in Chapter 6, in christian communities, recurring giving is called the tithe. What is unique about the tithe is the motivation and heart behind it. People in these faith communities don't tithe because of duty and obligation, nor because "it makes them a good person." The primary motivator behind the tithe is an acknowledgment that "what I have isn't mine; it belongs to God." The mindset behind the tithe is that those of us in the Christian faith return to God what is His anyway.

The lesson here for outside organizations is that because of the tithe mindset, Christians create a lifestyle of giving, where consistent giving is part of their everyday life. All nonprofits, whether faith-based or not, can learn from this first principle truth. The goal is to build relationships with donors where giving to the organization is incorporated into their lifestyle, from a place of gratitude rather than duty.

It is not only possible but essential to create a community that gives based on a sense of the purpose that it delivers to their life.

You do not build recurring giving based on a sense of duty or negative emotion such as guilt or obligation. Rather, recurring giving is built from your donor's gratitude for your organization, the community around your organization, and the fact that giving enables them to focus part of their life on something other than their own selfish needs.

Whether you agree with the church or not, creating a draw and opportunity for recurring giving is key to sustainable financial growth and can be employed by anyone.

For the church, the best way to invite people into recurring giving is to focus on principles by teaching and educating on the tithe. You can set your church up for success by allowing the congregation to automate their giving. Use a platform like Overflow, which lets your congregation donate on a recurring basis automatically, such as setting it up one time through the platform on a recurring schedule rather than having to make the decision and action every two weeks or every month.

For non–churches, focus on productizing recurring giving. Figure out what it means to accomplish something within your organization. For example, let's simplify and say that New Story Charity found it takes $12,000 to build a new home in Latin America. Expose that. A $1,000 recurring gift every month for 12 months means that a donor would be able to build a new home in a year. Someone may not be able to give $12,000 upfront, but they may be able to budget out $1,000 a month either alone or working with other members of their community.

Or scale it down. Let's say it takes $120 to build a well in an underserved community. That would mean that just $10 a month would allow someone to build a new well every year. When you productize your recurring gift, you tie the donor's contributions back to your organization's impact and create a reason for people to want to give to you month over month, year over year.

Cadence of Communication

Your organization needs discipline for how you update the community. With a strong vision on a clear time line with tangible impact and excellent execution, there must be a consistency in how the vision is being communicated to the community. Your organization should be regularly providing your community of donors with meaningful updates about the progress toward the vision.

This becomes even more important the less of a regular touch-point you have with your donors.

Organizations such as the local church or local community centers see their donors and supporters regularly, on a weekly or sometimes near-daily basis. This gives them an advantage in being able to build deep relationships within the community over time. For other nonprofit organizations such as museums, charities, or performing arts centers, who do not see their community on a regular basis, it is even more important to have discipline in maintaining regular communication.

Currently, many organizations rely on email communications to reach their community. But in order to reach your community, your organization needs discipline in how you measure the effectiveness of your communication over time.

Already, people are increasingly harder to reach via email. Email open rates are down, and younger donors lean on email less and less in many aspects of their lives. Is your organization making the investment in keeping up with the times?

Measures of Communication Investment

- Is your organization present on SMS?
- Are you present on social media, where wealthy tech millennials and the younger generation interact on sites such as Instagram, TikTok, and Twitter?
- Do you have an intentional communication plan on multiple channels?

This is not just about sharing your branding and broadcasting updates. The goal is genuine engagement that enables you to build relationships with your supporters. Whichever methods of communication your organization uses, treat those touchpoints like they are vital. Use them on a regular, consistent basis to deepen the relationships within your community and strengthen your supporters' ties to your organization.

Story and Testimony Driven

Alongside vision, for every ask you make to your donor community, you need to share 10 times the amount of stories and testimonies of the impact of your organization. The ratio cannot be one story to every ask throughout the year.

These need to be stories of transformation. These cannot be minor changes. These have to be transformative. A person, a city, a community was transformed in some way directly because of the efforts of your organization. Stories of transformation humanize and contextualize the impact that your organization has more than anything else.

The structure of the story can be gleaned from Hollywood. There needs to be a protagonist who is battling the specific problem or obstacle that your organization has professed to help overcome. The solution to this problem must come from your organization, and the story should build to a climactic, overcoming moment.

There are various ways to tell the stories of your organization's impact, such as via video or email or face-to-face at events. Incorporate these stories into your various forms of communication and into events. No matter how they're shared, the stories should be impactful. This is when your donor community will truly understand and see the impact of how their contributions to your organization are changing the world. Many people may not remember the details of what you said, but they certainly will remember how you made them feel.

Clear, Intentional Brand

Brand is not solely good design. Good design matters and should be intentional. But your brand is a set of actions that are reinforced over a long period of time. Your good design should be intentional, meaning there should be a reason that things you put out look the way they look. This communicates care and value.

The appearance of your brand communicates the care you put toward the area you're attempting to affect. If you don't value your branding, people interpret that to mean that you don't care about the impact of your organization. Perception is reality, even if it's far from the truth.

In this day and age, fundraising is increasingly personality driven. The idea of following and connecting with an institution is becoming less and less attractive, and people are increasingly drawn to a personality more than a corporate brand.

For example, although Charity:Water is an amazing brand, what initially built the brand was people's response to and relationship with Scott Harrison, the Founder and CEO of Charity:Water. In the church world, more people follow pastors' accounts than they do the church account. This doesn't mean that every organization's brand needs to be tied to one singular personality. As I'll discuss more in pillar number 10, the team can be the thing that makes or breaks a brand. And you have to take inventory of the team that makes up a brand when building a brand.

Whose actions drive your brand? The team.

The perception of your brand is based on your team and who that team is becoming. In a healthy organization and for a healthy brand, your team's actions should always tie back to the mission, vision, and values of your organization.

Are your mission, vision, and values intentional, consistent, being actioned in the behaviors of your team?

If the answer to any of those questions is no, then your organization does not have a healthy brand, and your community will sense it. Address those gaps with the team.

Then, ensure that you have a system to continue to reevaluate your mission, vision, and values, as well as the status of the previous questions, to ensure that your brand remains relevant and actioned.

Culture of Generosity

If vision paints the picture for our community of where you want to go, culture is the vehicle that determines how you get there. What type of vehicle is your organization?

Figuring out the vehicle you are will determine the speed at which you go. This involves evaluating your methods, your mechanisms, the ways you communicate, every way your company shows up. What you want to create in your organization is a culture of generosity.

A culture of generosity is very different from a culture of giving. Many organizations have a culture of giving. A generous culture is extravagant, sometimes to the point of being irrational. A generous culture is lavish. It is something that leaves an unmistakable memory or impression that says, "Wow, I cannot believe I got to be a part of that." When you have built a culture of generosity, people will be willing to go to great lengths to see a project fulfilled and impact happen. It is on a level that is so great that it can inspire a whole community and compel a whole room. They will fight to see your organization's mission accomplished.

This is the kind of generosity that you should be working to build: a culture where people are willing to sacrifice something and bring in their whole family to give to the mission. When your community has this culture, asks like recurring giving feel like effortless decisions, and members of your community actively seek out additional ways to give more to be part of the vision. The type of generosity where people creatively think of ways to give, and ultimately make giving part of their lifestyle, leads to sustained giving and sustained impact.

If you want a culture of generosity, you have to articulate what that means in the context of your community. For example, in VIVE Church we have a culture of generosity that is centered on big, audacious faith. Our community operates from a fundamental belief that our vision is always going to exceed our resources. We will always operate in a level of stretch and sacrifice on a personal level because our first principle is that God will meet us in sacrifice. Therefore, our community continuously gives generously because we teach, preach, reinforce, and celebrate that there is a blessing in sacrifice. There is an appetite in our community shown through our supporters' generosity. They want to give more, pour out more, and celebrate opportunities to give to our mission.

The takeaway here is that what you model within your community will determine what the culture will become. This is not built in one-time interactions. Within our community we model generous, enthusiastic giving again and again. We share stories within our community that reinforce this culture. Our community reinforces this culture member to member to the level where the culture of generosity is tangibly felt within our community, and there is an appetite for more generosity. The end result is not just consistent, but increased generous giving.

Intentional, Aligned Team

Team is one of the most underestimated keys to building excellent donor relationships. Many times leaders within an organization believe that as long as they follow the principles described in this chapter they will build a top donor experience. But a leader can envision what they want the donor experience to look like, can be confident in how the vision and execution is communicated, and can even be proud of the brand, but if whoever is responsible for collecting the gift does so in a way that is off culture or off brand or poorly executed, people leave their experience with the organization with a bad taste in their mouth.

For example, let's say your organization's vision is to eradicate food insecurity in an impoverished community. You have set a goal to raise $10 million, and you are now inviting donors to be a part of this by next Friday. You've expanded your donor options to include not only cash but also stock and cryptocurrency. You've laid out the incredible, billion-dollar impact that this $10 million will have, and donors know that when you reach this goal by next Friday, you will start to deliver on your plan on a clear time line. People in your donor community have seen you execute on your vision in the past, they get regular updates from you, and they have been able to see stories of transformation from past work you've done battling food insecurity. Your community has a strong culture of generosity and wants to give to make this happen. You've created an excellent giving event where someone has committed to giving $10,000.

There are several roadblocks that will start to erode trust. Let's say that a $10,000 giver has committed to giving stock because the person on stage said that your organization can receive stock. If that person is not provided prompt communication and taken care of with a seamless way to donate that stock, the moment that was supposed to be a blessing for this person, because they get to participate in this exciting project, turns into a burden. If the process includes the finance person telling the donor to fill out forms, fax in forms, or email back and forth with their broker and takes 45 days, you've now added stress to the donor in executing that $10,000 gift. While you still may receive this gift, reluctantly now, by the donor, you're likely not getting this person's $10,000 next year.

Or let's say that this person wants to give $10,000 in cryptocurrency, and your finance team has handled it quickly and given them a link to a platform like Overflow, which makes this seamless. But by the time they're ready to click the link to transfer some Bitcoin, Bitcoin has dropped to half its value, and this person has just lost half of their net worth, so now they want to give $5,000 instead of $10,000. Now, the person on your team facilitating the transaction doesn't understand the context of the market and isn't prioritizing the relationship, so they make this donor feel bad. They treat this like an invoice situation rather than celebrating the gift that can still be given. Again, whether you get $5,000 or $10,000 from this person now, you will never get another dollar from them again.

Even if most of the touchpoints the donor has with your organization are good, if givers are not provided prompt communication and provided with a seamless giving experience, the moment that should be a blessing is instead a burden.

If your organization's process for collecting finances and the necessary follow-up communication takes too long, while you might still get the money for your current campaign, you're not getting it in the future.

Does the person handling your donor experience give grace and celebrate gifts given, even when circumstances may change? If someone begins the process of giving to your organization but due to cold feet or changing circumstances decides to back out, how they are treated determines whether they will ever consider giving to your organization again. Even if they choose not to give now, it is important that they are met with gratitude and understanding in alignment with your organization's values to ensure that they return to give in the future.

Does the person handling your donor experience understand shifts in the market? For the noncash donations we've discussed—cryptocurrency and stock—shifts in the market may mean that the cash value of a donation has the potential to shift drastically between the initial commitment and the donation being received. The person responsible for collecting these donations needs both knowledge and sensitivity to ensure that they are providing an informed donation experience to the giver that encourages them to give this way in the future.

Framework and Foundation

The 10 principles discussed in this chapter lay out the framework and foundation that will give you the best opportunity to maximize giving by providing your donors with an experience that draws them in and keeps them engaged and generous.

Now that you have a deeper understanding of what can improve the donor experience, we are going to go straight into how to maximize the most important time of year for most 501(c)3 organizations, which is year-end giving! In Chapter 8 we break down the tactics to ensure you capitalize on a time of year that people are most willing to give, and give big.

8 | Maximizing Year-End Giving

Year-end giving is a pillar of the nonprofit financial strategy. The idea of year-end giving closely parallels the Silicon Valley mentality for fundraising. In Silicon Valley there are multiple rounds of fundraising: pre-seed, seed, series A, B, C, D rounds. Fundraising in Silicon Valley is typically done with a very specific process.

The process is typically two to four weeks or, for a larger round of fundraising, two to three months. Within that time, an organization has a very specific plan to meet with a specific set of investors. Beyond raising the necessary funds, the goal is to create what's called FOMO (fear of missing out) and buzz within the overall tech community. This enables these expanding businesses to consolidate their time and create an intense period when they are focused on fundraising.

In the same way, if nonprofits were to have a fundraising round it would be most aligned to the year-end giving cycle. The end of the year is when most of the momentum is. Any nonprofit organization that wants to increase their funds needs to create a catalytic moment—a moment that spurs people into action and encourages them to give abundantly.

You want to create atmospheres of generosity and build a season of momentum when everybody is giving together. There is no better time than year-end giving for nonprofits.

Many organizations create too much pressure around year-end giving by leaving the planning until too late or planning ineffectively. Your end-of-year giving strategy should not be a cause of stress when handled correctly. If your organization has done the necessary work to build relationships and donor buy-in from your community from January through September, then October through December you should be operating out of the overflow of the year's work. Before focusing on this chapter, make sure you've used the tools in Chapter 7 to build your overall donor experience.

Once your donor experience is locked in, this chapter has actionable insights to maximize the success of your year-end giving event.

How Do You Maximize Your Year-End Giving Event?

This chapter is meant to be a practical playbook for any head of fundraising, event coordinator, chief financial officer, nonprofit board, or anyone responsible for budget and event organization.

In order to meet or exceed your goals, you must be intentional about how you plan your event. Be sure that you are planning specifically to address the following areas to maximize year-end giving:

- Begin in alignment
- Select the guests
- Organize the venue
- Content and agenda
- Build anticipation

Begin in Alignment

One thing that's really important to understand no matter what industry or sector you work in is that you go further, faster, and are more effective when you're aligned with the leader of your organization.

If you're reading this book, you're probably responsible for a fundraising goal, but you may not be responsible for casting the vision of your organization. To achieve your goal, it is really important that you are in alignment with your organization's leader on what the vision of the organization is. If you are not 100% sure of what your leader sees as the vision and purpose of your organization, get this alignment before pursuing anything else.

Many times, a leader will cast a vision at a very high level. It is your responsibility to be the implementer, integrator, and interpreter of their vision. Take time to ask clarifying questions and add detail to take your leader's vision from dreamscape to landscape. In other words, you must take the vision from a high level and break it down into pieces of communication that can be more easily disseminated to your donors and supporters.

As an example, many pastors will tell their team about their vision to buy a church building one day. The interpretation of that vision is understanding what type of building, what location, why does the church want a building, what will be done in the building—all detail-oriented clarifying questions. Asking why, what, how, and other clarifying questions will enable you to take a vision and articulate it in a way that you can explain it to the people who have the means to give.

An example of detailing out a vision for a building could be the following:

Our vision is to purchase a building in the heart of the Silicon Valley because it will represent permanence, laying a stake in the ground and our commitment to serve this city for the long term. This building will be a hub of activity, full of life all throughout the week. Sunday worship experiences will simply be just one of the many activities in this building that facilitate community, connection, and transformative moments. During the week there will be a world-class cafe with high-speed internet where people from all over the SF Bay Area will want to visit, work from, and take meetings in. There will be an innovation wing where the hottest start-ups in the area that are mission-focused will call home and be a central place of operation for their staff. A fully accredited college will host courses, lectures, and practicums in the main auditorium and all throughout the building. There will be a recording studio for musicians and artists to produce art and albums. The venue as a whole will be a highly coveted event space where the most exciting product launches and meetups will desire to be held. All of this is in alignment with being a light in the community and a place of connection and transformation!

This vision statement for a building is an example of how to articulate a vision for a place so that people can start to imagine it!

Start here, because everything else you decide for your year-end event should flow from this vision.

Select the Guests

If you're not intentional about who you're inviting to the year-end giving event, whether it's digital or in person, your gathering will have zero impact. You need to have a filtering process to decide who in your community you will invite to your event. Your guest list will affect so many of the other decisions you make about the event.

At VIVE Church on an annual basis, typically in November, we host what we call our Vision Gala. Choosing the beginning of November for the event is very intentional so it doesn't compete with Halloween, Thanksgiving, or Christmas, while still taking advantage of the year-end giving momentum. Placing it in this time frame also enables givers to hear the vision, commit, and prepare over several weeks to fulfill their gift before year-end.

Our guest list for this event is derived from the people in our organization who have given over a certain threshold in the previous 12 months. Those people are sent a specific, personal invitation from our lead pastor and CEO of our organization to come to an exclusive, invite-only event, our Vision Gala.

We're explicit about what the night is. Attendees know that this is not just a night to dress up for a nice meal or date night setting. They know that this is a night where we're making a financial ask for them to partner with next year's vision. So our filtering process means that we're inviting people who have already shown that they're a supporter of our organization at a high level and are opting in to being asked for money, which is really crucial to ensuring that we have the right people in the room.

We have specifically chosen the threshold of giving that earns people the right to attend our gala based on the needs of our organization and the ask we will be making the evening of the gala. Everyone in the room that night will be in the top percentile of our givers and therefore likely able to give generously that night.

The threshold you set for the givers within your community will give you a benchmark of how many members your event needs to serve. This will really inform the style of your event.

Consider what the size of your invite pool means for your event organization. For example, at VIVE our threshold leaves us typically with 500 to 1,000 people. That matters, because that informs our style. We know that in this range we can still do a physical event with round tables and seat a leader at every table.

No matter the event, you want every attendee to have the opportunity to connect with a leader from within your organization. You want a leader per table facilitating conversation: connecting with the community and making sure the conversation at each table is fostering generosity and gratitude to the organization and reminding everyone of the results your organization has achieved. Make sure the ratio of leaders to guests is thoughtful. You will then need to take adequate time to prepare the chosen leadership team to support at the event.

You will want to set up the seating in a way that will inspire maximum generosity. Though presumably everyone in the room is a strong giver, you may choose to honor your biggest givers. At VIVE Vision Gala, we seat our biggest givers together at the front of the room, but there are several ways to honor your biggest givers regardless of the format of your event.

Often, major donors don't seek public recognition but really appreciate private recognition. So any way that you can connect the founder, CEO, or leader of your organization directly with the major donors can be quite powerful.

Here are some ways you can honor major donors:

- **Exclusive information.** Major donors love being part of the process. If they're finding out about a vision element at the same time everybody else is, that's not honoring. It's a great honor to be able to have exclusive information early. We call this the meetings before the meeting. You should aim to have 25–50 "meetings before the big meeting" which serves as momentum towards the event.
- **Personalization.** If you have let's say 25 major donors in your organization, do you understand how they receive recognition and honor? Everyone is different. In the context of marriage we consider the five love languages (touch, words of affirmation, acts of service, quality time, and gifts). It's the same way with your relationship with major donors. You need to build the relationship to the level that you know what you can do to make them feel valued.
- **Big vision.** Many times major donors get unlocked when the thinking is really big. If the thinking is too small, that's the best way to limit their giving. Their giving starts becoming unlimited as the vision becomes unlimited. And the best compliment you can have for a major donor is to expect much from them. They love accepting and rising to challenges.

Consider carefully the people you are seating together at your event. Will they be able to connect with each other and have a meaningful conversation? Will they be sitting with like-minded people who can inspire each other to give more generously?

The idea is that the people you seat together will inspire each other and connect with each other and that the people at your event will walk away with new friends. If people from your community connect and become friends at your event, they're going to feel grateful that they attended, and your event will forever be tied to a positive memory.

There is a really important principle and phenomenon in Silicon Valley called the *network effect*, which is a phenomenon whereby increased numbers of people or participants improve the value of a good or service. For example, as more users post content on Twitter, the more useful the platform becomes to the public.

Taking this same principle, if there is no intentionality in seating and people are simply there to watch and listen, there is no additional value with each person added to a table. But if you create cross-connection moments in your seating choices, you are establishing a mini network effect in real life. This can be accomplished digitally as well.

At VIVE we experienced this during the pandemic, when we were running the first-ever global Vision Gala completely online. There are various software programs out there, even Zoom, where you can facilitate connection elegantly online. One option is to use breakout rooms.

Carefully craft the different topics of the breakout rooms you're sending guests to pre and post your vision presentation so you can provide a more intimate setting for conversation. This takes your event from a broadcast, where your donors are passively consuming, to an engaging experience, where they truly feel like they're in community. Your guests still get to see each other and connect with other guests and with your leaders on the topics that are important to you and to them and that drive that spirit of generosity.

At our church, we centered the breakout rooms on topics such as location, people in the marketplace, ministries, and other segment-oriented topics. That's one way to make a bigger setting, even if it's online, seem smaller and filled with intention.

Organize the Venue

You have to understand, contextually, how you want to actually raise the year-end money for your organization. Some of the most effective ways of raising money involve creating a space for a catalytic moment.

To give abundantly, people need to be in an atmosphere of generosity and abundance.

Our VIVE Vision Gala has such an atmosphere. Vision Gala is a black tie event, and guests are served a three-course meal. We put a lot of value on the way the event looks and feels because the aesthetics communicate value back to our donors, which puts them in a setting to hear, receive, and digest our vision and encourages a response.

What does that look like for your organization? You have to clearly define what your setting is and what that space needs to be to produce the momentum for your big ask.

Now we get into the tactical. Once you have done the work to put together your guest list, you can select your venue. You want to select a venue and a decor that create an x factor moment for guests and make them want to be generous. Don't look to cut costs here.

You need to consider the logistics of how your guests will experience the venue. How are they going to get to your event, and how will they feel when they get there? What will traffic be like for guests coming to your venue? Will they be driving far or through slowdowns that will cause them to arrive frustrated? What is the parking situation at the venue? Will they be frustrated because you chose a trendy venue, but you didn't think about the parking situation, so by the time they walk in they are late and stressed? How far do they need to go from where they park to enter the venue? Are you choosing a venue with proper climate control, or will your guests be distracted all night by being too hot or too cold?

Is your venue the appropriate size for your number of guests? You don't want a venue you're drowning in. A room that feels empty doesn't create a sense of momentum. But you also don't want a space where there's no room to move around or connect. The size of your venue is very important.

After choosing your venue, create your decor plan. First impressions are everything. There are whole books written on the importance of first impressions. Within my team, we use the Coke bottle analogy. If you take a Coke bottle and undo the cap and let it sit, what happens? It goes flat. I've never met a person who wants to drink a flat Coke. Why? The ingredients are the same, the look is the same, nothing has actually changed about the Coke except that it's no longer fizzy. What does that mean? People don't buy the Coke because of the ingredients; they buy it because of the fizz. That's the same way people will interact with your catalytic event. What fizz moments are you planning for?

Although your content is important, your guests won't remember all of it; they will remember the way you made them feel. Consider the many touchpoints you have to draw them in. What do your table settings look like? Do you have seating charts and name settings on each seat well placed? Are you providing a flow that takes donors on a journey starting at the door, telling stories along the entryway about the impact your organization has had? Do you have a setting that inspires conversations that highlight your impact throughout the night?

All of your venue and aesthetic choices need to be oriented toward cultivating an atmosphere of generosity.

My wife and I recently attended an event called Messenger Cup where the venue selection, aesthetics, and intentionality in the experience was top notch! Their mission is to bring biblical teaching to everyone, including those in remote areas with no access to resources or the bible translated in their language. "Because everyone deserves to know." When we walked into this beautiful banquet hall at the Broadmoor in Colorado Springs, we were greeted with a nice photo op (which was shared with us immediately after the event so we can post about it and share it with the world). And when it came to finding our seat, there was a takeaway element next to our table seat number and name. It was a figurine, and you received a boat, jeep, or plane. Based on that figurine, the team directed you to an experience and that experience would lead you on a travel journey either through the pathway mode of a boat, jeep, or plane, illustrating that they will use any means necessary, whether it's water, land, or air, to be able to get resources into the most remote places of the world. They illustrated this with a designed experience and by the end of the path you were met with a big wall of impact: all of the places and people they have reached over the years and what that has done to transform communities. This is all before we even had taken our seats!

The intentionality of the venue, aesthetics, and design all pointed toward the impact of the organization and put you in an atmosphere of inspiration and generosity.

If your vision is to hold your event online, there are a lot of elements you can incorporate to grow the event and cultivate a generous atmosphere.

When you're doing online events and you want to create a culture of generosity, there is much more prework involved. The success of your event is going to come from minimizing the level of surprises on the day of the event by stacking things in your favor in the lead-in time. Use the weeks leading up to your events to get loose pre-commitments from your community. You want to go into the event with a strong understanding of who is committed to showing up and giving on the night.

One element that will be crucial to build attendance for the event is the mastery of how you tell stories on social media.

Another key element that will enable you to gauge those pre-commitments is your ability to create peer-to-peer environments in anticipation of the event, for example:

- Online breakout sessions for like-minded guests to connect
- Master classes on subjects related to your mission or areas of interest for your community
- Facilitating one-on-one or small-group meetups in anticipation of your event with staff or leaders within your organization

Again, the goal is to go into your event with a strong sense of the level of possibility from the event, so that you're not surprised on the day. This event should be the cherry on top of the work you've done to encourage year-end giving. You want to stack it so that the night of giving feels like your organization is building forward momentum, rather than the event being disappointing because you've missed a mark or missed a goal. The prework of the smaller gatherings alert you to whether you're going to make your goal or if there is more work to do to build generosity within your community.

One example of how to determine pre-commitments leading up to the event is to start coining different levels. For example:

$1000 giving level = core
$10,000 giving level = influencer
$100,000 giving level = legacy

In conversations leading up, you can invite people to share what level they would like to come in to support the vision, which helps set expectations and create momentum.

Specifically, for an online event, what's really important outside of who's invited is to ask them to dress up and prepare themselves as if they are going to an actual event. This puts them in the position to be front-footed and leaning into the event, rather than back-footed or passive. Make it fun. Have them take a photo and share it in a community forum or post it on social media with a specific hashtag.

Another way to increase the presence of the event is to introduce a draw card. This can be a prominent or influential figure, someone beloved within the community, or maybe even an athlete or respected celebrity who's aligned with the mission and the vision. A lot of times people will dial in if they know there's something to dial in for and if you create exclusivity in the invitation. For example, an app called House Party took off during the pandemic because they hosted digital, exclusive house parties where people could enter a video chat room and connect with a celebrity. An element of exclusivity coupled with a draw card can really drive the growth of an online attendance.

Content and Agenda

You've optimized the venue and guest list; now it's time to organize the night. As you are building the flow of the night, remember that you are aiming for a catalytic moment, which can be defined and distilled in the coordination of your reveal. If you give information too early, or hold information too late, you dilute the opportunity for this moment of momentum.

A catalytic moment can be engineered through a tiered rollout of information. Begin with your key staff: the people who are actually going to make this vision happen. Invite them into the process of shaping it and figuring out how to roll it out. From key staff you go to your board, because your board needs to be involved and committed to the vision and the ask as well. They typically overlap with the major donors, which would be the next tier. As stated previously, you honor your major donors when you let them know the big vision and the ask ahead of everyone else.

The content and flow of your catalytic event are crucial. Be sure that you are constructing this presentation with your leader. Your presentation needs to be compelling, concise, and clear.

We call this order of events the *run sheet*. You need to structure this night like a movie, with an introduction and welcome, a build, a climax, and then a reprieve where people can non-emotionally commit to giving.

Start first with reflection.

Be really clear with your guests about everything that happened the past year—at VIVE we call this our year-end review. Did you do the things you said you were going to do last year? In what time line? What was the impact? How is that aligned with your mission, vision and values? How is that reinforcing the driving mission and vision you've been communicating?

Emphasize and reinforce your impact by tying it back to your mission, vision, and values. This puts people in a place to celebrate and also puts them in a place of gratitude. When people are in a place of gratitude, they're more willing to give or give again. That's where this night has to start.

Make sure storytelling is incorporated. Whether it's a live testimony, a video story of the impact, or something else, you want to take your high-level statistics and numbers and turn them into names and stories. Go from the high-level macro view of your major metrics and big numbers from the year and create a story that contextualizes them to a person who's been affected. This story should be personal. At the end of the day, people connect with people and stories. Whatever methodology you choose, convey a very distinct story that is relatable or further illustrates what the organization does.

You're building a story arc. So you start with the warm-up via the year-end review. You build with the storytelling and personal testimony. Now, you're at your climactic moment, which is the vision pitch and the big ask.

To reiterate from Chapter 7, the vision pitch needs to be on the level of a billion dollars of impact. It needs to be something that challenges and stretches people, in fact, I dare say, something that intimidates people.

That's the only way you inspire big giving. If the people at your giving event feel that the vision is possible without them, you won't unlock big giving. But if they feel they need to give for the organization to even have a shot to achieve the vision, that's how you unlock their participation.

You also need to be bold about your ask. Your ask needs to come with a spirit of invitation, not desperation. The people at your event should feel so lucky to partner with your organization because it will give their life vision and purpose.

If you have rolled out your ask correctly ahead of time, this moment will be especially powerful because you already have a percentage of the room on board. With the first two steps of the run sheet you've already led people toward the impact, and then in this big moment you set people's sights on the future vision. If you have 20% of the people on board and already anticipating the big reveal, it heightens the atmosphere of the room.

Choose the person making the ask carefully. Their perspective cannot be that the donors are doing the organization a favor. The mentality has to be that the organization is doing the donors a favor. This ask is not because you need the money. Your organization will be doing these initiatives whether the people in the room choose to give or not, because you're all committed to finding people to resource the vision. These donors are the lucky few that get to be in the room to hear the vision and contribute first. Your attendees will not experience the fear of missing out! The sense in the space should be that your organization isn't desperate for their money, but rather that the donors feel a need to give. In Silicon Valley terms, they get to be in the earliest round of investment, which is always the most coveted stage to be in.

Invitation is better than desperation, because desperation creates the wrong dynamic. This is human psychology. If you see a person on the street and you start running after them, what are they going to do? They won't run toward you. They'll run away from you.

You need to understand that you have something that donors want to run toward. You have something that will provide them with purpose. You have something that is worthy of inviting your community to give to. The person who is making this ask should not feel or convey that your organization has to chase after your donors. Givers just run away from that. They need to create the atmosphere that is inviting the people present to join in and give.

Now, tactically, make it clear that there are a lot of options to give. Platforms like Overflow allow your organization to confidently say that you can give a wire transfer or give from your stock portfolio or via cryptocurrency. Make the options clear so that your guests know there are a lot of options. Awaken their imagination on how they can give.

At the end, create a reprieve so that the moment is not about emotion or manipulation. When it is time for your guests to donate, give them time to pause thoughtfully and consider whether they will give. You don't want this moment to be at the peak; you actually want it to be the wind down.

If a commitment is made because the person was drinking too much at the event, or based on the emotionalism of your presentation, or based on being swept up in a moment, then the pledge they make on that night is not going to be fulfilled. And if it is, it will be met with regret, and they will not want to do it again. You want your givers to have a sober understanding of what they're committing to, and that will minimize the discrepancy between commitment and fulfillment.

Build Anticipation

Now, you've selected the venue, constructed the run sheet, and you're working on the presentation and creative assets. As you build up to the event, consider how you're going to get people excited and in a place of anticipation for the event.

The base of the strategy is to ramp up your communication as you approach the event. Start by sending one email three months ahead, then one two months ahead. One month ahead, send one email a week, and the week of the event, send daily communication if you can, leading up to the event.

Marketing is all about frequency and recency. You want to increase communication more as you get closer to your event to take advantage of how people's brains work: to take advantage of recency bias. Something that you just saw or something that was just communicated to you will remain top of mind, so as you increase communication as the event draws near, the event will increasingly remain top of mind for your guests. Frequency plays into this as well.

The reality is that it takes multiple touchpoints for the message to actually be received and remembered. So you want to make sure you have both frequency and recency, especially leading up to the event.

From Chapter 7, remember that you have other forms of communication as well. Consider the platforms that your invitees may be using, such as texting, and how you can integrate those to provide additional touchpoints with your giving community.

From a branding and design standpoint, be very thoughtful with the choices you make to tie your communications to your event. At VIVE, everything we create for the Vision Gala is tied to our big reveal of our vision on the day of the Gala. We tie in our social media designs, the assets that we use for our email newsletters and everything about the look, the feel, and the language is tied to the big reveal on the day of. It's a subconscious way to begin telling the story before the event arrives. We're using our communication ahead of time to tie in the big reveal, the vision, and what the big ask will be.

To do this at scale, you need brand guidelines solidified within your organization. Do you have them? Figures 8.1, 8.2, and 8.3 shows what Overflow's looks like.

To wrap this up, what's important to understand is that for most organizations, more than 60% of your budget will be made up in your year-end giving campaign—in your catalytic moment. Unless you are doing everything and implementing all of these best practices to maximize this moment, your organization will really miss out on the biggest tailwind of giving within the year.

It's easiest to be able to raise money toward the end of the year. There's so many implications here that are connected to year-end giving. There's momentum from people earning year-end bonuses.

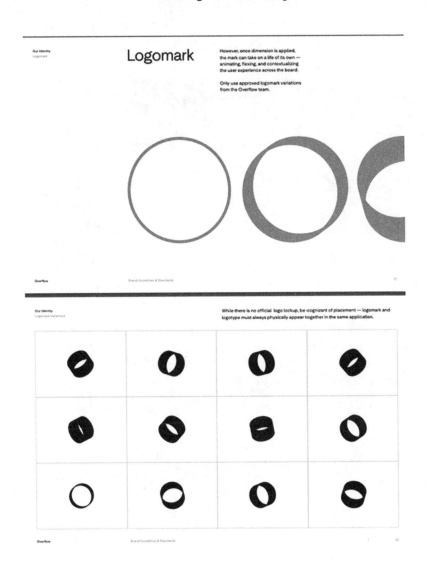

Figure 8.1   Overflow branding guide

Source: Overflow internal resources.

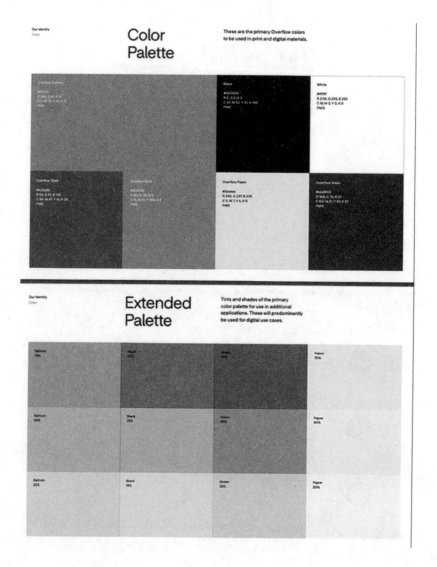

Figure 8.2   Overflow color palette

Source: Overflow internal resources.

People are searching for year-end charitable tax deductions. You can even benefit from just being aligned to the holidays when people are in a more generous, giving mood. These are just some of the reasons that maximizing the moment is so important.

Figure 8.3 Overflow photo direction
Source: Overflow App, Inc..

If you fail to maximize your year-end contributions, you will face an uphill battle for the rest of the year and will start from behind in the upcoming year.

Now that we have given you a lot of playbooks, tactics, and guidance, let's dive into real-world examples in Chapter 9 with organizations that are finding incredible success implementing many of the concepts we have covered in this book thus far!

9

Examples of Successful Organizations Unlocking Unprecedented Levels of Generosity

I've spent eight chapters giving you principles, playbooks, best practices, deep dives, and master-class-level tactics on unlocking new levels of generosity. The best thing I can do from here to conclude this book is to give you real-life examples of our customers who have applied some of the concepts in this book and have seen a great impact.

This means if it can work for them, it can work for you. You just need to work it!

The six examples I've chosen will enable you to see a diversity of organizations (based on region, size, and type) that have all found success through the principles in this book.

- **Oceans Church.** A Southern California–based church plant that used the methods from this book to raise $400,000 in a matter of weeks.
- **RIP Medical Debt.** A New York–based national nonprofit that went outside the box by incorporating stock donations and is seeing a massive return.
- **Reality SF.** A Bay Area church that streamlined their donor experience and saw massive return without needing more funds.
- **OnDeck.** A Silicon Valley incubator that incorporated a foundation to further their mission of providing tactics for success to ambitious founders.
- **Hope Village Church.** A young Seattle church developing a congregation that embraces new ways to give and is seeing transformative results.
- **Overflow for Corporations.** I'll break down how the core principles in this book have been able to help two for-profit companies as they work toward social impact.

Oceans Church

When you picture Orange County, California, you probably imagine pristine beaches filled with skinny palm trees or surfers ready to catch the next big swell. Or perhaps you think of Disneyland or the show "Laguna Beach." Despite the abundance of attractions, Pastor Mark Francey saw a different picture when he looked at Orange County.

As a native of Southern California, Francey was well aware of the touristy charm of the area. However, he knew that even a city that seemingly has "everything" still has a deeper hunger for hope. After taking a trip with his wife, Rachelle, when they returned to the area, their hearts soared with confirmation that they were to plant a church there. In 2018, they uprooted their lives to lean into their calling.

Stepping out in faith, they planted the seeds for what would now become Oceans Church: a community that would be a refuge for a tired and busy region to hear the message of Jesus and find a sense of belonging. Through the pastoral work they poured into their community, Francey and his wife were able to grow their congregation. But this brought a new challenge.

Oceans Church reached the point that they needed a new building, and this required a higher level of fundraising. As Francey himself noted, building campaigns, fundraising, and managing finances are some of the less glamorous aspects of church planting. Pastors are often prepared in terms of prayer, scripture, and preaching, but they often are caught off guard by the extensive logistics that go into it:

> I didn't realize becoming a pastor was going to be so involved with other things other than the bible and prayer. . . For some reason, I thought maybe being a pastor was loving people and praying and reading my bible, and that was going to pretty much encapsulate my job responsibility. I had no idea that I was going to be an expert in real estate land acquisitions, working with cities, working with fundraising events. I had no idea what I was signing myself up for.

Scaling requires generosity, and Francey and his team were looking for a way to maximize that. That's when they were exposed to the power of noncash asset donations. For Oceans Church, the tides changed when they partnered with Overflow to receive both stock and crypto donations.

Some of what holds pastors like Francey back, even when they become aware of new options on the table, is the concern that their community won't respond to or use alternative options. But Francey was exposed to the idea when he heard me on the Carey Nieuwhof Leadership podcast (episode 472) and became intrigued.

Francey knew that if he wanted to integrate stock and cryptocurrency giving, he needed to focus on the donor experience for his congregation. He needed a solution that provided a user-friendly giving platform that was accessible and easy to use. Even if people are massively generous, they can get caught up in the weeds of how to give.

The average attention span in 2022 is not very long, and people are quick to discard anything that's confusing or clunky to use. However, if that initial interest or spark can be tapped into quickly, you're more likely to absorb their attention and trust. Francey noticed this as well, which is why he also chose to partner with Overflow after contrasting it with the "traditional" way of stock giving, which is a lengthy process.

Francey's commitment to broadening the scope of how his congregation can give has paid off. Within just a few weeks, Francey reported that the church saw almost $400,000 come in via stock and cryptocurrency. What was key is specifically exposing this option to their high-potential and high-capacity givers, whom they call *kingdom builders*. Making sure that the core group especially knew about this was important to the success of this campaign.

After his experience with stock and cryptocurrency giving, Francey and his team are believers. They see noncash asset giving as the key that will open up major giving avenues for not just their church, but for all churches. With more and more people diversifying their portfolios with stock and crypto, having a service to accommodate said donations becomes a huge priority.

"I just think that it's going to be more and more utilized as we see time progress. More people are carrying so much of their assets in their stocks. A lot of people even nowadays carry a lot of their assets in digital currencies. So I'm really excited to be able to introduce this to . . . our people in our church. But also, I think the body of Christ can benefit," Francey said.

Overall, what we can see from Oceans Church is that no matter where your organization is in its growth journey, there is money to be unlocked from focusing on streamlining your donor experience and opening your giving options to include alternatives to cash gifts.

RIP Medical Debt

Imagine that you finally get the surgery you need. You've been waiting months, and the life-changing procedure opens up a world of possibilities. Until it doesn't. That relief can quickly disappear after receiving a steep medical bill.

For 79 million Americans, this is a daily reality. Medical debt is a crushing weight that puts a strain on finances, relationships, and everyday life. Either you take on debt or you don't get the help you need. It's a lose-lose.

RIP Medical Debt, a New York–based, national nonprofit, is making sure people aren't forced to choose between good health or financial stability. When debts go unpaid, some hospitals and doctors sell them to collections companies. These companies buy up the debt for a fraction of its face value, yet attempt to recoup the full cost. Fueled by charitable donations, RIP Medical Debt buys existing medical debt on the secondary debt market at a huge discount.

They abolish the debt completely, and then send out letters to people informing them their debt has been completely wiped out.

RIP Medical Debt already had several of the benchmarks of a strong donor experience. Their vision is tangible, clearly communicated, and has an impact that directly ties to donor funds. Their execution is phenomenal, and on their website you can scroll through personal stories of people expressing their immense gratitude for this service. As one couple put it, "We almost cried when we realized the letter was real." When VIVE Church partnered with them, we were able to see their culture of generosity and the alignment of their team firsthand.

Their donor experience is clearly working for them. In fact, they've wiped out nearly $7 billion dollars in medical debt to date. Yet, given that RIP Medical Debt is funded by donations, they were still searching for more ways to maximize their giving intake so they could in turn maximize their impact. When I met Scott Patton, vice president of development at RIP Medical Debt, he was intrigued at the possibility of implementing a more streamlined, accessible system to manage donations and open the door to alternative forms of giving.

As we've discussed in this book, making donations via stock has not historically been an easy process. It can involve back-and-forth contact with the nonprofit, the brokerage, and the donor. The unnecessary extra steps only lead to more frustration and precious time spent.

Oftentimes donors want to give but aren't sure how to initiate a transaction or how the overall process works. The more resistance and confusion, the less likely it is people will give or feel confident in their giving. As Patton said, "We had donors. I mean, I would have half a dozen inquiries [saying] 'hey, where can I send this or make these stock donations?' I would say that it was marked first by being under-resourced from a time perspective and then being under-resourced from a communications and transparency perspective."

However, when Patton and his team realized how much they were potentially leaving on the table, they invested in Overflow as the right tool to cut past the frustration and deliver results. With the means to collect stock donations unlocked, Patton was careful to communicate about this new tool without overwhelming or confusing the organization's donor base.

In this case, the marketing aspect to inform donors about stock giving has been mostly digital, because it provides a quicker follow-up for people to ask questions and get informed.

"We use digital [communication], because we can send a series of follow ups and include Overflow. I want to remind donors about the benefits of stock giving," Patton said.

Though the marketing process is still being shaped and refined, it's evident that the results have spoken for themselves. While more "traditional" givers (who tend to give large stock donations) have been hesitant to stray from the way they've always given stock, statistics show that an overwhelming amount have been receptive to the new option.

Per Patton, more than 70% of donors are giving through their new platform, and the average donation is $16,000. These large stock gifts have helped further RIP Medical Debt's mission of knocking out big chunks of medical debt while keeping their organization running smoothly.

The considerable amount of stock donations that have come in help further RIP Medical Debt's mission to be a "force for systemic change."

Reality SF

San Francisco is one of the most expensive cities in the United States. As such, families and individuals need to keep pace with rising costs, such as home/apartment rents of more than $4,000 a month for a single bedroom. Churches and nonprofits in this city, therefore, also must navigate this increasingly tricky financial landscape.

As an organization that relies primarily on donations to run, how do you not only survive but also thrive in a city like this? Money can be a touchy subject, especially in the church world, but it's a necessary conversation in a city like SF, where many people say churches come to die.

For Reality San Francisco, a church located in the Mission District, the opposite has happened. They're more alive than ever. Reality SF has been a fixture in the Bay Area church scene since 2010, when it was established as a church plant. The church had already said yes to stock donations using the "traditional" method. Then Tarik El-Ansary, administration and finance pastor at Reality, heard about the possibility to streamline and expedite noncash donation collections from Scott Harrison, founder of Charity: Water.

Despite being a bit hesitant about branching into and investing in new pathways, El-Ansary and his team recognized that the benefits outweighed the initial costs and would alleviate headaches brought on by the previous stock giving process. They were looking for a "high visibility, reputable, excellent service provider to handle stock donations."

To keep up with growth, El-Ansary and his team partnered with Overflow to pave new pathways of generosity by streamlining how easy it is for their donors to give. Empowered by early results with stock donations, they quickly took it one step further by adding the option to give crypto as well.

Despite not heavily emphasizing giving or finance to the congregation, Reality SF has an abundantly generous community. In the last three years (despite a pandemic and unstable economy), their giving has steadily increased from $5 million in 2019 to $6 million in 2021.

But their investment in technology to make noncash giving as easy as cash giving yielded, and continues to yield, transformative results. Prior to Overflow, their biggest stock donation year on record was $225,000. Within less than a year of working with Overflow, the stock giving total had more than doubled to $500,000. An already generous church community, in just eight months, Overflow helped facilitate and bring in over half a million dollars in stock and crypto giving.

Even without a strategic marketing plan in place, the church is averaging stock donations of $15,500 via their new, streamlined giving platform. That level of capital will only boost future projects, such as their recent building campaign. This increase in donations has enabled Reality SF to further their impact in their community. As a church, they decided to buy an existing church building previously owned by Bethel Church on the corner of Valencia and 24th St.

In a city where church buildings are often converted into recreational spaces, Reality SF wanted to reestablish the presence of the church and steward the space for maximum community impact. They desired to maintain and expand a food bank that operates out of the building space, start a center for Christian thought and practice, and open the doors daily for those seeking a quiet, peaceful refuge from the city.

Beyond building campaigns, the church is excited about having a reliable platform to hone the appreciated wealth and generosity of a high-income, urban area in order to better serve the neighborhood and meet needs in the city.

OnDeck

OnDeck (beonddeck.com) is a Silicon Valley incubator that encourages founders to grow from pre-idea to fundraise, supported by their community of founders. They provide services and resources for entrepreneurs, founders, or aspiring founders to be able to accelerate their idea into an actual start-up, launch the start-up, and fundraise.

However, in order to provide these services, OnDeck has an entry cost. In their process of selecting the founders they wanted to partner with, they found that they had to reject some ideal founders because the OnDeck program cost a few thousand dollars (at the time about $2,000, now about $3,000) and some talented founders didn't have that money. Whether they were recently out of school, or struggling to raise capital, founders from a certain background, life stage, or region didn't have access to capital like other founders might have.

OnDeck saw this problem, and they wanted to work with Overflow to start a foundation, which they called the Access Initiative. We helped them launch a philanthropic arm to their for-profit business, and the Access Initiative housed scholarships for under-estimated, under-represented founders who otherwise wouldn't be able to afford OnDeck.

What's really cool is that this foundation is funded by alumni from this incubator. People would go through the program, get equipped with the resources from OnDeck to be able to find a cofounder, start a company, get funding, launch the product, recruit top talent, become successful, and because of that success come into some money. Then they would, similar to a college, give back to the program through the foundation, essentially allowing OnDeck to form an endowment.

Through the work we were able to do with them and this unique offering we were able to provide, coupled with good marketing and good placement on their website, good rollout on Twitter and Instagram and LinkedIn and all of their social media networks; in the first few months we were able to raise $1 million for this scholarship program. We have turned it into an endowment that has become a cycle of generosity—as more alumni come through they're refilling the endowment, which is then deployed toward up-and-coming founders who can't afford the program. A good proportion of those founders then become successful, and the cycle continues.

Imagine if OnDeck didn't create this foundation. They would be so limited in the type of people whom they could accept. By broadening the scope of the people they can accept, they end up with a higher probability of producing the best founders and entrepreneurs.

The cherry on top to all of this is that because OnDeck used Overflow for their online cash processing, they minimized their processing fees due to the platform's direct partnerships with certain payment facilitators that enable them to secure the best rates.

On top of being a strong philanthropic angle for the organization, this initiative also meets their bottom line and makes their business even better. They capitalized on something universities have figured out for decades, which allowed this organization to work out a new avenue to greater success with us.

This $1 million is just the beginning. We're on track to do much more than this in the future as they continue to grow, fueled by the principles from this book.

Hope Village Church

This next example focuses on a church that sought to do something many would consider impossible: planting a church during a pandemic. In March 2020, Hope Village Church began with the mission to bring the message of Jesus to the Seattle area. The year proved to be challenging but didn't shake the calling of lead pastors Drew and Emma Davies.

The Davies were used to overcoming great challenges—and great distances—in their pursuit of being church builders. The couple relocated 7,200 miles from Brisbane, Australia, to San Diego to be a part of a church plant, and then were led to Seattle, despite warnings that it was a historically difficult environment for ministry.

The Davies stayed firm in their mission and have seen considerable fruit from their commitment and perseverance, but there are still logistical, financial challenges that come from being in an expensive, rapidly growing area home to tech giants like Amazon and Microsoft.

"I think one of the fundraising challenges we face, which is unique to the Greater Seattle area, is just the sheer expense of what buildings cost up here. We're not looking at buildings that are $1 or $2, or even $3 million. Buildings up here are upward of $15 to $20 million or more," Drew Davies said.

Nonetheless, the Davies stayed firm in their mission and have seen the fruit of doing so, as they have a place to gather, a thriving congregation (with more than 500 in attendance each Sunday), and a bright future. And that future is even brighter when they were presented with a pathway that could make the fundraising process a whole lot easier.

By amplifying their giving avenues, the church has been able to fully lean into their mission of permeating every sphere of Seattle and "being a village that walks with you through your valleys and celebrates with you in your victories."

Drew and Emma Davies were sold on expanding their giving options, but they first needed to test the waters and see how their community would respond. Presenting something new to your congregation or organization can feel uncomfortable. In the church world, many have a specific view of how giving works, such as dropping dollars in a bucket or writing a check. Instead of being seen as a helpful tool, donating cash/debit/credit through an app can feel intimidating, foreign, or even unnecessary.

Drew Davies knew from the beginning that his congregation and the church's mission would benefit from stock giving but wasn't positive what the response would be. To his delight, the community was extremely receptive: "We weren't sure whether we'd have a handful of donations. From the very beginning, we saw that people were open to giving through stocks, and some of them love it. Some of them have actually switched their giving from regular giving to just giving on stock so that it works better for their taxes. When it's easy for people to give, that's really an important thing for us."

Due to the high proportion of the stocks being given connected to technology companies and other Fortune 500 companies, there has been incredible opportunity for corporate gift matching as well. This serves as an additional multiplier to the unlocked generosity through stocks.

One of the biggest aspects that stood out to both the Davies and the community was how simple and easy it could be to collect these donations. They did extensive research before deciding to partner with Overflow, and it proved to pay off, as donations started flowing in from day one.

In just two years, Hope Village Church has seen and felt the impact of opening up new channels for their growing congregation to support the church. It's enabled them to both have a space to meet and accomplish their goals. Drew Davies spoke earlier of the logistical and financial challenges of being in a city like Seattle. With some of the figures that have been brought in so far, the church is looking more like the thriving, dynamic village it set out to be.

And although he preferred not to disclose numbers, Davies hinted at the deep success and benefits they've seen on a financial level.

Overflow for Corporations

We recently launched Overflow for Corporations, a product aimed at the for-profit sector. We've taken the principle of generosity and what we've been able to unlock on our platform, and we've contextualized it for corporations' social impact arms.

Many corporations have social impact departments, sometimes under human resources or government relations or even marketing communications. What these companies are realizing is that their employees want to have a greater meaning and purpose to their job. If these companies can align their team with deeper purpose and meaning, the result from their employees is higher loyalty, deeper engagement, and more fulfillment at work.

One of the ways that they do this is through corporate social responsibility and social impact. They will create programs such as corporate matching programs where they will empower their employees to give to certain organizations, and up to a certain amount, they'll match the donation. In many cases this means they're doubling employee's charitable donations within the year through funds given on the corporate level.

Another thing they'll do is partner with a nonprofit organization. They'll feature the nonprofit and donate products, services, time, or even mobilize employees to come behind the nonprofit financially through employee giving programs. Many times they choose nonprofits whose values are aligned with the corporation or with the values of the leadership team.

Our platform helps accelerate and amplify these measures, because we provide so many ways beyond cash giving to be generous. Companies have flocked to this new platform because they understand the power that outside the box, future forward thinking unlocks to further increase employee engagement and unlock generosity within their corporation.

I have two specific examples I want to share with you.

Twilio Unlocks Generosity Within Their Community

Twilio is a publicly traded company, an important software company based in San Francisco. Twilio calls themselves the future of communications, and they serve other companies in more than 180 countries around the world, with teams of employees in at least

20 countries. This is a company with a massive global impact that sought ways to improve its social impact as well.

Twilio has a social impact arm of its business that invites employees to give money to social causes within their communities. Its impact fund has multiple methods of grants and investment to support nonprofits and social enterprises, resulting in accelerated impact through innovative communications technologies.

Twilio is also one of the early adopters of Overflow Corporations. When the head of social impact at the time met with us, she shared that her whole mission, her whole goal, is to increase the amount of giving and specifically the amount of giving per employee in the company.

At the time, before they opened up their platform to support multiple methods of giving, the average gift was under $50.00. At that same time, the stock price for Twilio was more than $200. Just imagine this—the head of social impact promotes Overflow within her organization, educating employees about the software, and even based just on tax benefits alone an employee decides to give one share. That's already four to five times more than the average cash gift.

Choosing multiple noncash asset donation options enables the organization to multiply the impact of its individual gifts. Adding more options, and educating its community about the benefits, meets the social impact goal. It can, and has, successfully encouraged more giving per person, because it found a way to unlock people who wouldn't have given to give now because they have a unique way to do so.

In just the first few months, Twilio was able to raise over $100,000—and that was pre-matching. Once some of that is matched by the company, it becomes hundreds of thousands of dollars going toward more than 50 nonprofit organizations. Beyond the financial impact, 50 high impact organizations tackling issues such as social injustice, food insecurity in the local communities, clean water, and software education in resource-poor neighborhoods, all received surprise gifts on behalf of the Twilio employees. That is really, really cool!

Amplitude Leverages a Conference to Give

Amplitude is a public company focused on analytics products. They call themselves the gold standard for product analytics, and they serve multiple Fortune 500 companies across various sectors, providing products that turn user data into meaningful insights. In particular, Amplitude hosts a conference every year called Amplify that brings together thought leaders from multiple fields to share powerful insights in the product and growth space.

When they heard about the mass shooting at Robb Elementary School in Uvalde, Texas, in May 2022, the Amplitude team was moved to think about how they could respond. They knew they had their Amplify 2022 conference coming up, and they understood the power of leveraging a conference event to raise funds for a cause.

However, they didn't just want to ask conference attendees to toss a couple of dollars in a box on the way out. Instead, they reached out to Overflow and asked us how they could leverage this conference to create true impact.

We were able to work together with their team to provide their CEO with an Overflow link and a QR code that could be leveraged throughout the conference to provide attendees with multiple ways to give.

On a personal level, this was a massive win for our platform. In Chapter 6, I mentioned that companies are always looking for ways to get in front of their target customers. For us, this was really great product placement and created a good catalytic moment because they had all their employees, partners, and vendors, thousands of people, in one room, as well as a broadcast streamed online.

From a learning standpoint, one takeaway here is to make sure you're increasing the reach of the events and conferences you put on by streaming the event online. There are platforms as simple as YouTube that you can use to increase the reach of your events. When you have valuable information to share, and a valuable platform to promote, you want to make sure to spread your message as far and wide as you can.

Beyond just featuring the QR code, during the conference Amplitude's CEO spoke about how the shootings in Texas really moved them and then shared about how that motivated them to partner with an organization called EveryTown to pursue ending gun violence. That message was shared to the thousands of people in the room, and the thousands more watching digitally, paired with a QR code that made it very easy for people to stop and give cash as well as assets.

In just a few hours, we raised over $43,000 directly for pursuing efforts to stop gun violence.

These are just two examples of incredible, billion dollar companies that, like you, are working to unlock generosity using the principles in this book. Although these stories come from my personal experiences as the CEO of Overflow, beyond the utility of my platform I hope they encourage you to think bigger about the power of what the principles in this book might unlock in your organization. Whether you're trying to build a church or a nonprofit, there is more available for your organization when you expand your thinking past the way you've currently been doing things.

Each of these case studies focused on a team with an incredible mission and showed how embracing noncash assets, powerful fundraising principles and the right fintech platform enabled them to fund that mission. Your organization has an incredible mission. Are you evolving and embracing the new so that you can fund that mission?

10 | Unlocking Generosity Wrap-Up

One of the things that really attracted us to Silicon Valley and has kept us here is this almost irrational sense of optimism. In the religious space we call it faith. In Silicon Valley it's called risk. Generally, what's so attractive is the limitless nature—this idea that we can create a future better than what we have in the present.

This takes visionaries, courageous people, who are willing to risk and stretch and have a deeper purpose and meaning for their life. That's what's so powerful about Silicon Valley, and I would argue this is the same type of spirit that some of the best nonprofit leaders, creators, makers, and fundraisers have.

If you're working for a nonprofit, a charitable organization, or a church, you are either a visionary or a vision carrier of your organization. We hope that this book has provided an environment where you can think bigger. In our current society, it's possible to unlock unprecedented amounts of generosity that have never been available before.

In this last chapter, I want to give you a high-level summary of the ground we've covered and give you an example showing that if I were to start a 501(c)(3) organization today, how I would approach it. Using the principles laid out in this book, I'll walk through how I would apply the various learnings to unlock unprecedented generosity for my organization.

What We've Discussed

We started the book by talking about how in the past decade it's been evident that giving has gone online, and as this has occurred there's been more focus on the user experience. Because of Silicon Valley, online transactions via companies like Amazon have become pervasive in our lives. Not just the things we buy online, but now through apps, the internet, and the online environment, we also book our cars through an app, we book our accommodations through online marketplaces like Airbnb, the list goes on and on, and in every case the user experience is so important. Giving has been no different.

The simultaneous trend is that giving has started to go noncash. We saw that in the examples of DAFs in Chapter 1. And yet, although giving has gone noncash, noncash has not gone online. So the powerful combination of noncash giving and it going online with a good user experience is going to be an explosive formula. It has already been explosive for so many organizations that have caught on to this.

You combine this double-thread with a triple-threaded chord, which is this massive shift of generational wealth from boomers to the next generations, and the way millennials think about money as a way to extend their identity, and we see investing happening more than ever before. With the different emerging investable trends, you can basically invest into anything—art, wine, collectibles, and so on. But what people are really investing into are crypto and stocks. In Chapters 4 and 5 we did a deep dive into how to understand those two specific noncash asset classes, and how you set your organization up to be able to maximize those for donations in the immediate term. What we learned is that as there is more investors and appreciating assets, there is more opportunity for these appreciating assets to be donated to nonprofits!

Alongside an understanding of how to capitalize on investing trends, you can also apply master-level tactics for fundraising. It's not just about unlocking net new giving, but how do you become more efficient and effective with giving overall? How are you minimizing your processing fees? How are you teaching the concept of tithing or learning from the principle of the tithe? How are you identifying high-capacity givers who are not yet giving? How do you make sure that across all of your giving that you're taking advantage of corporate matching benefits, free money that you do not want to leave on the table? How are you making sure you're talking to all generations? When we think about IRAs, wills, trust, and legacy giving, this is not just about the next generation of giving, but we must also speak to the current generation of givers: boomers.

All of these things are very important, but the most important thing is that you have your vision right, your communication right, and that you have a year-end giving campaign that is clear and consistent year over year.

Your consistency will create a compounding effect. Don't get discouraged if you're applying some of these principles in year one and you're not seeing the results that you hoped for. That doesn't mean you should give up; it means to iterate and be consistent. The compounding effect of consistency year over year can also be exponential. In the Silicon Valley we call it Product-Market fit (PMF) which is a concept where you continue to iterate until your solution starts to serve the market at scale. Once you have PMF and a consistent way distribute the product, you start having exponential results year-over-year.

The Nonprofit Example (Overflow Nonprofit Resource Center)

Now, let's imagine that I'm starting a nonprofit today—let's call it Overflow Nonprofit Resource Center (ONRC). Here's how I'd describe it:

> *Overflow Nonprofit Resource Center (ONRC) exists to be a hub for leaders of nonprofits, churches, and charitable organizations to get equipped and empowered with free resources to launch and grow their organizations. This nonprofit resource center wants to serve as a place where world changers, leaders of social impact, and visionaries at 501(c)(3) organizations can go and get all of the resources they need: everything from how to start a nonprofit including legal resources, to figuring out how to build a team including organizational tips to set up a staff, to the playbooks for running a gala and the giving technology stack, and everything in between.*
>
> *The mission of (the fictional) ONRC is to increase the philanthropic pie to a trillion dollars by 2032.*
>
> *There are two paths to achieve our goal. The first is to increase the number of nonprofits, causes, and leaders in this space that are compelling and that are actually solving pressing problems. We aim to increase the amount of these great*

social impact organizations with big vision. The second is to equip current nonprofits to be even more effective in addressing the problems they aim to solve.

The vision is that every high-impact nonprofit with the right mindset would have an overflow of resources to accomplish the mission and vision that they have set out to accomplish.

Just imagine this future. Imagine a future world in which you can see some of the most ambitious founders wanting to solve things like homelessness in our cities, food insecurity, or the need for clean water. What if they had the appropriate amount of resources to fund the solutions they already have? They're already solving these problems on a micro-level; we aim to provide the means for them to scale to solve problems on a macro-level.

You can see here how I start with the mission and the vision. I start with the why: an orientation of *why* we exist as an organization, *what problem* we aim to solve, which in this fictitious case is the lack of resources and tools in the nonprofit marketplace, and because we exist, *where* we want to go. If you do not have these foundational pillars set up, start there. Whether you are a 30-year-old organization or a one-year-old organization, it's always good to renew and refresh your understanding of these pillars.

Once you get these pillars right, then it's about making sure these pillars are communicated throughout all your communication channels. Your biggest front door is probably your website. The prerequisite to having a good website is to understand your brand. For ONRC, I would invest into branding: the look and feel of our site down to the level of our typography consistency, the color palette, and the way that we use language and messaging to reinforce our mission, vision, and brand promise.

I would make sure that every employee, every staff member, and every volunteer understands the brand proposition, because the brand is not just a look and feel, it is reinforced by a set of actions. I would make sure that's consistent at every point, the things an outsider can see and feel when they interact with the staff. Consistency needs to be locked in across the website, the social media channels, and any piece of communication whether a newsletter, an email, or text message.

How are you making sure that your messaging appeals across generations? How are you making sure that you're not just talking to the boomer or Gen Z, but that you have a space and a place that communicates unilaterally. I believe that you can create multigenerational communities. I believe that you can engage a whole community. But what's important is that in the immediate term, you're engaging boomers as your current source of wealth, but you're not forgetting Gen Z, the next generation of wealth that will be the most generous generation this world has ever seen.

For ONRC, I would make sure that we were really smart about it. So when we're messaging, I'd remember that boomers are looking for legacy, while millennials and Gen Z are looking for identity. So I'd consider how our messaging addressed both of those core motivations.

So far, for ONRC I have my pillars, I'm extending it into a exercise to solidify my brand and create or refresh my website, I'm making sure the brand is consistent across social media and all other communication channels, and I have a strategy for every single generation. Now, I need to make sure my toolkit and my platform can support the vision.

So I'm going to be going with a giving platform that is able to unlock every single asset class, one that doesn't just reduce my cash processing fees, but can also unlock stock and crypto gifts. For the older generation I'm thinking about 401ks, IRAs, mutual funds, while for the new generation I'm thinking about tech stock, cryptocurrency, and even other alternative assets. I want to make sure that the giving platform can support everything we're looking to do in terms of engaging multiple generations and all asset classes.

Then I'm going to get really good about community building. I want to make sure I'm defining even the subsets within the ONRC community. For the ONRC, the way that we can define it is core, creator, and catalyst. Core are people willing to give $100 or more within the year. Being a creator is giving over $1,000 a year. Being a catalyst is giving $10,000+ within the year. How do I actually solidify these communities?

Each tier should come with a new set of benefits. I would think about the benefits of each of these tiers within the community. What do you get at the core level versus the creator level versus the catalyst level? I also want to make sure that each tier understands their impact.

- At the core level, you are a part of the really important team giving to the core operations of the organization. You get insight into the collection of organizations that ONRC supports, and you get exclusive volunteer opportunities to be part of the impact and part of the change.
- As a creator you are underwriting the start-up costs for a whole nonprofit to get off the ground. You get invited to exclusive events for a subset of nonprofit organizations where you can have experiences that no other donors get to have.
- As a catalyst you're helping a nonprofit to be able to scale their existing impact 10 times more than what they're doing today due to the resources we're able to provide them. You get a curated experience at a concierge level to be able to really feel like you're an extension of the team and see that you have direct impact. For example, let's say New Story Charity is an organization that we support, and their mission is ending global homelessness by 3D printing homes, which is amazing. What if a catalyst actually had an annual curated experience to go to Latin America where they're printing these homes and got to have dinner with some of the families that were housed that year?

  This is the type of experience you get as a catalyst, and creating experiences like this would allow ONRC to develop excitement and anticipation for reaching this tier and building deep community. As a catalyst you would look forward every year to going with a similar cohort and meeting new people to join you on these excursions and missions. These trips are not only a really fun adventure but also provide deeper meaning and purpose to your life, as well as lifelong friendships and relationships.

This is an idea of how I might create tiers and community cohorts within our ONRC givers and our supporters. And I would maximize our giving through all of the different tactics I've outlined throughout this book.

I would make sure that our donors knew that the most efficient way to give, if they're giving cash on a recurring basis, would be to give via ACH. I would push everyone to give via ACH to minimize their processing fees, and I would be transparent with them about how much we save as an organization when they choose ACH.

I would encourage, and make it seamless and easy, that people take advantage of their corporate matching and really emphasize that this is money left on the table if they don't. Many work for Fortune 500 companies like Apple, Google, or Facebook that match sometimes up to $10,000 or $20,000 per year. I would make it so easy for them to go through the steps of setting it up and working with their HR team, providing email blurbs and using platforms like Overflow that automate and streamline this, and then direct them to the systems they might be using such as Benevity to give insight into where to go and what to look for. All of this to make sure that our givers can take advantage of the money on the table.

I would push a noncash asset–giving strategy. I would make sure that the options for noncash giving were emphasized within my nonprofit communications. As we know, 90% of wealth is in noncash assets, so this needs to have parity with my cash strategy. I need to be talking about noncash as much as I talk about cash. I'll provide callouts and FAQs of the tax savings benefits on my website. I'll have noncash giving buttons at parity with cash buttons on every giving page. There's going to be equal opportunity and options to give noncash assets as there are for cash, because I know if I can influence and encourage them to give noncash, that gift is likely going to be more generous. The Overflow platform specifically sees an average of $128 cash donations but over $10,000 average noncash donations, so I know the importance of focusing on encouraging noncash assets.

With my boomer donors, specifically, I'd be educating them about the need to take a required minimum distribution and making sure that if they don't need it all, they know they can use some of it for good while getting a charitable tax deduction. This is a win–win situation for them, and I would make sure that our organization was taking advantage of that.

For ONRC to thrive, I would make sure that engagement with our givers and supporters was our top priority. I would make sure that there were monthly events available for them to be a part of and that they can go to any of our ONRC hubs in major cities.

These would be inspiration office-like spaces where they could go to connect with others, a watering hole for people to make some connections, get work done, get a coffee from a cafe, and be able to book and rent a room. A physical space where people could gather and gain value, part of the reason they're a contributor. To further differentiate my tiers, maybe at the creator and catalyst levels you get free desk space or free private space when they pop in. This would be a place where entrepreneurs, investors, and social impact leaders can gather together—a cool, innovative space where community is made.

I would make sure that our physical hubs had monthly events, whether a happy hour, or a lunch and learn, or a dinner event where they can meet nonprofit industry leaders. I'd bring together corporate leaders in the for-profit space with social impact leaders in the nonprofit space. Panel events, where people can learn and be inspired. The goal would be to have these events on a monthly basis, if not a weekly basis.

We'd have a huge fundraising gala every single year in November: a flagship one in our main location, the San Francisco Bay Area, and distributed ones in all of our other major city locations. This big fundraising gala would use all of the principles we talked about in Chapter 8.

Remember, these are some keys on how to maximize year-end giving:

- Begin in alignment with the vision.
- Select the guests intentionally.
- Organize the venue around inspiration.
- Create a communications strategy, run sheet, and agenda that builds anticipation.

As you can see from my fictitious example along with our real case studies in Chapter 9, this is all very attainable for you and your organization. You can do it! I want to note that every step that I'm outlining for ONRC may not look the same at every step for your organization. The key is that you contextualize the steps for your organization, mission, objectives, and location!

I've had the privilege to talk to hundreds of nonprofit leaders at this point, and the biggest lever to unlock unprecedented amounts of generosity—more than the tactics, principles, context, and education I provide in this book—comes down to one thing: dream bigger. That is my biggest piece of advice to move the needle for you.

Dream bigger. Think bigger. Push yourself to achieve more within your organization. You'll often find that when you ask yourself the question, how do we increase our impact 10 times, you will then be able to increase the amount of money you'll raise 10 times to get to that impact.

A key in the Silicon Valley that I've learned is that Silicon Valley investors and venture capitalists reward ambition! Billions of dollars are released every year toward companies that will probably not work out. But they get a chance because of their ambition and vision. You are not a "probably not". You are a proven solution! Communicate vision and dream big!

References

Chapter 1

Define Financial. (2022). *Charitable giving statistics for 2022.* https://www.definefinancial.com/blog/charitable-giving-statistics/

Double the Donation. (2022). *Nonprofit fundraising statistics* [updated for 2022]. https://doublethedonation.com/nonprofit-fundraising-statistics/

Fidelity Charitable. (2022). *What is a donor-advised fund (DAF)?* https://www.fidelitycharitable.org/guidance/philanthropy/what-is-a-donor-advised-fund.html

National Philanthropic Trust. (2021). *The 2021 DAF report.* https://www.nptrust.org/reports/daf-report/

Chapter 2

Bader, L. (2019). Millennials: How to cater to the most generous generation. *Forbes.* https://www.forbes.com/sites/forbesnonprofitcouncil/2019/07/05/millennials-how-to-cater-to-the-most-generous-generation/?sh=3e585bf0253a

Chapkanovska, E. (2022). *19+ Massive millennial spending statistics.* https://spendmenot.com/blog/millennial-spending-statistics/

Coindesk. (n.d.). Bitcoin. https://www.coindesk.com/price/bitcoin/

Double the Donation. (2022). *Nonprofit fundraising statistics* [updated for 2022]. https://doublethedonation.com/nonprofit-fundraising-statistics/

Gogol, F. (2022). *Study: 94% of crypto buyers are gen Z/millennial, but gen X is outspending them* from https://www.stilt.com/blog/2021/03/vast-majority-crypto-buyers-millennials-gen-z/

Insider Intelligence. (2022). *34 million US adults own cryptocurrency.* https://www.insiderintelligence.com/insights/us-adults-cryptocurrency-ownership-stats/

OpenInvest. (2021). *$30T in inheritance moving to millennials: How to prepare your business for this great wealth transfer.* https://www.openinvest.com/articles-insights/how-to-prepare-for-the-great-wealth-transfer-to-millennials

Scientific American. (2010). Generosity might keep us healthy. https://www.scientificamerican.com/podcast/episode/generosity-might-keep-us-healthy-10-10-26/

Scott, E. (2020). *Helping others can increase happiness and reduce stress.* https://www.verywellmind.com/stress-helping-others-can-increase-happiness-3144890

Smith, C., & Davidson, H. (2014). *The paradox of generosity: Giving we receive, grasping we lose.* Oxford University Press.

Smith, J. M. (2014). *Want to be happy? Stop being so cheap!* https://newrepublic.com/article/119477/science-generosity-why-giving-makes-you-happy

Srinivas, V., & Goradia, U. (2015). *The future of wealth in the United States mapping trends in generational wealth.* https://www2.deloitte.com/content/dam/insights/us/articles/us-generational-wealth-trends/DUP_1371_Future-wealth-in-America_MASTER.pdf

Suttie, J., & Marsh, J. (2010). *5 ways giving is good for you.* https://greatergood.berkeley.edu/article/item/5_ways_giving_is_good_for_you

Parker-Pope, T. (2020). The science of helping out. *New York Times.* https://www.nytimes.com/2020/04/09/well/mind/coronavirus-resilience-psychology-anxiety-stress-volunteering.html

Chapter 3

Board of Governors of the Federal Reserve System (2021). *Survey of consumer finances and financial accounts of the United States, 2021:Q1.*

Newbery, E. (2022). *Binance CEO says LUNA collapse left him "poor again."* https://www.fool.com/the-ascent/cryptocurrency/articles/binance-ceo-says-luna-collapse-left-him-poor-again/

Sigalos, M. (2022). *Homeless, suicidal, down to last $1,000: Celsius investors beg bankruptcy judge for help.* https://www.cnbc.com/2022/08/02/celsius-investors-owed-4point7-billion-beg-judge-to-recover-life-savings.html

Yates, J. (2021). *90% of the world's millionaires do this to create wealth.* https://thecollegeinvestor.com/11300/90-percent-worlds-millionaires-do-this/

Chapter 4

Crypto.com. (2022). *Crypto market sizing report 2021 and 2022 forecast.* https://crypto.com/research/2021-crypto-market-sizing-report-2022-forecast

Double the Donation. (2022). *Nonprofit fundraising statistics [updated for 2022].* https://doublethedonation.com/nonprofit-fundraising-statistics/

Fidelity Charitable. (2021). *Growing popularity of cryptocurrency could fuel charitable giving.* https://www.fidelitycharitable.org/about-us/news/growing-popularity-of-cryptocurrency-could-fuel-charitable-giving.html

Gemini. (2022). *2022 global state of crypto.* https://www.gemini.com/state-of-crypto

The Giving Block. (2021). *The Giving Block 2021 annual report.* https://thegivingblock.com/annual-report/

Hoss, S. (2021). *The future of giving: Trends shaping next-gen philanthropy.* https://www.forbes.com/sites/forbesnonprofitcouncil/2021/12/27/the-future-of-giving-trends-shaping-next-gen-philanthropy/

Moraes, M. (2020). *8 modern tips for marketing to millennials.* https://blog.hubspot.com/marketing/marketing-to-millennials

Chapter 5

Anspach, D. (2022). *Annual stock market returns by year.* https://www.thebalance.com/stock-market-returns-by-year-2388543

Axelrad, C. (2018). *Does your nonprofit promote stock gifts? You should! Clarification.* https://clairification.com/2018/10/11/nonprofit-promote-stock-gifts/

Board of Governors of the Federal Reserve System (US). (n.d.). *Households and nonprofit organizations.* Retrieved from FRED, Federal Reserve Bank of St. Louis.

Caporal, J. (2021). *Study: What are gen Z and millennial investors buying in 2021?* The Motley Fool. https://www.fool.com/research/what-are-gen-z-millennial-investors-buying/

Fidelity Charitable. (2016). *The giving gap: Donor awareness and use of strategic giving methods.* https://www.fidelitycharitable.org/content/dam/fc-public/docs/insights/the-giving-gap.pdf

Fidelity Charitable. (2021). *The future of philanthropy.* https://www.fidelitycharitable.org/content/dam/fc-public/docs/resources/2021-future-of-philanthropy-summary.pdf

Nonprofits Source. (2018). *The ultimate list of charitable giving statistics for 2018.* https://nonprofitssource.com/online-giving-statistics/

Planned Giving. (n.d.). *7 reasons donors stop giving.* https://plannedgiving.com/wp-content/uploads/7-reasons-donors-stop-giving.pdf

Russell, J. (n.d.). *Cash is not king in fundraising: Results from 1 million nonprofit tax returns.* https://www.pgcalc.com/pdf/ExecutiveSummary.pdf

Statista. (2021). *Monthly downloads of the Robinhood app worldwide 2018–2021.* https://www.statista.com/statistics/941809/robinhood-app-monthly-downloads/

Vogels, E. A. (2019). *Millennials stand out for their technology use, but older generations also embrace digital life.* https://www.pewresearch.org/fact-tank/2019/09/09/us-generations-technology-use/

Chapter 6

Double the Donation. (n.d.).
Kehl, F. (2022). *The complete guide to understanding credit card interchange rates & fees.* https://www.merchantmaverick.com/what-are-interchange-fees/

Additional Resources

For direct fundraising tips, best practices, and access to our team, text "high-growth fundraising" to +1 (253) 316-8510.

Additionally, as a reader of this book we are offering free access for 12 months to our Fundraising Leadership Forum, where you will have exclusive access to the top fundraisers in the world alongside their content, such as closed-room video events, in-person gatherings, and a library of recordings. To redeem simply email `flf@overflow.co` with subject line "high-growth fundraising" and include your full name and a selfie with your book in the body of the email. Let's unlock generosity together!

About the Author

Vance Roush is the founder and CEO of Overflow and on mission to inspire the world to give. Specifically, Overflow unlocks unprecedented levels of generosity by empowering nonprofits, foundations, churches, and corporations to accept noncash assets like stocks and crypto with ease. Ninety percent of wealth is in noncash assets and orgs are still mainly fundraising for cash. Overflow is fixing that. Through Overflow, its customers, and other endeavors, Vance has been a part of raising hundreds of millions of dollars to date from donors and investors and has dedicated his life to help others unlock generosity for their mission.

Outside of Overflow, Vance serves on the board of various nonprofits tackling society's most pressing problems and venture funds that deploy capital into underestimated founders. He also serves as executive pastor at VIVE Church and is a founding member. His background is in tech from companies such as Google. He and his wife, Kim, live in the Silicon Valley with their four children Lennox, Emerson, Tatum, and Wesleigh Dior.

vanceroush.com

Index